THE
LORD'S
PRAYER
DECODED

UNLOCKING A
LIFE OF PURPOSE
AND FREEDOM.

BRADLEY KENNETH LITTLE

©2025 by Brad Little

Published by hope*books
2217 Matthews Township Pkwy
Suite D302
Matthews, NC 28105
www.hopebooks.com

hope*books is a division of hope*media

Printed in the United States of America

First paperback edition.
Paperback ISBN: 979-8-89185-303-4
Hardcover ISBN: 979-8-89185-150-4
Ebook ISBN:979-8-89185-151-1
Library of Congress Number: 2025930129

"While the Lord's Prayer is seemingly familiar territory to many followers of Christ, Brad Little plows new ground by suggesting that it not only contains the key elements of a God-honoring life but also introduces the themes elaborated upon by Jesus in the remainder of the Sermon on the Mount. His perceptive – and at times, provocative – exposition of this famous prayer highlights the importance of forgiveness for those of us called to reflect the moral perfections of our Heavenly Father before a watching and spiritually needy world. Such an emphasis is especially timely in an age where the church is seemingly being influenced more by worldly values, attitudes, and practices than by those of the Kingdom of God, compromising the credibility of our gospel witness."

Randal Roberts
D.Min. President Emeritus, Western Seminary of Portland, OR

"I love this book! Brad Little shares insights and truths that gave me a new perspective and renewed appreciation for Jesus' temptation experience, The Lord's Prayer, and The Sermon on the Mount that follows. Like a single diamond has many facets to be appreciated, Brad shares a view of these passages that reveals both truth and beauty. His work is fresh, relatable, and readable, with life application for both new seekers and seasoned followers of Christ. It's a must-read!"

Vern Risner
Lead Pastor of First Baptist Church - Pekin, IL

"In more than three decades of preaching and teaching, I have never seen the whole text of the Lord's Prayer tied together with such clarity. When so many view the traditional elements of Christianity as antiquated, Brad Little brings a fresh perspective on a prayer that has far too often become a thing of nostalgia rather than a guide to a God-honoring life with our Father who art in Heaven. This magnificent work will pave the way for the intimate walk with the Lord we've all desired since conversion and does so within the framework of a prayer many of us have had memorized since childhood. Not only is *The Lord's Prayer Decoded* well worth the read, but it will change your entire view of the Lord's Prayer and the sermon Jesus taught to explain it."

James Perry
Lead Pastor, Creekside Baptist Church, Marion, IA

"At first glance, you might be slow to pick up another book on the Lord's prayer. I so wish that I had understood the broader narrative at play over my years of teaching through this prayer. Brad does a masterful job in helping us see through the baptism and temptation of Jesus, just how this prayer was displayed in Christ's incarnation and so is central for us. You will learn the theological truths at work that amid your own calling and temptations, this prayer reveals, amongst other things, the source of your identity, freedom from anxiety, the vitality of forgiveness, and resilience through temptation. This prayer opens the window for us to see that we are not left to work this out alone but in the context of the manifest presence of our heavenly Father."

David Whitaker
President, Venture Church Network

"*The Lord's Prayer Decoded* by Brad Little is a book of theology on prayer and a practical discipleship tool. Brad does a great job helping us get a perspective on why the Lord's Prayer will revolutionize your prayer life. Step by step, Brad visits each part of the prayer and asks key questions for application. These steps then get orchestrated together like the "Karate Kid" when he pulls all the disciplines of Karate into a full Karate posture; Brad then helps the readers to orchestrate the elements of prayer to work together to enhance your relationship with your heavenly Father. This book will help you in that process with the content and well-placed questions for application. Enjoy growing deeper!"

Dennis Blevins
Navigator, Ministry Coach

"By helping the reader understand a familiar passage in its greater context, Brad Little provides a greater understanding of what it means to find the purpose and peace that are so often missing in our turbulent world. His perspective on the Lord's Prayer within the context of Jesus' temptation in the wilderness and the Sermon on the Mount gives a clear picture of God's call to live in humility and forgiveness. The more believers grasp these concepts, the more they will have deepening relationships with God and others—with eternal implications."

John Craft
D. Min. Regional Executive Director,
Rocky Mountain Church Network

Table of Contents

Preface

I have always believed the Lord's Prayer offers us more. It's widely acclaimed as magnificent, yet I mostly encountered it during formal occasions. Some churches recite it regularly, others seldom or not at all. For some, it serves as a direct prayer; for others, it is merely a teaching tool. Despite its apparent simplicity, the prayer carries a deep mystique and is the sole instance where Jesus explicitly taught his disciples how to pray.

Jesus' decision to embed this prayer within the broader Sermon on the Mount narrative undoubtedly adds to its value. However, the prevailing notion that the segments following the Lord's Prayer are just a collection of unrelated topics feels overly simplistic to me. Reflecting on the depth of Jesus' wisdom, I became convinced that he wouldn't introduce this prayer without fully explaining its importance. It dawned on me that perhaps the discussions in chapters six and seven were his way of elaborating on the prayer.

My perspective was profoundly shaped during a moment at Western Seminary when Hadden Robinson commented on these very texts at the annual Lectureship Event. His casual remarks in our homiletics class mirrored the ideas I had been pondering. Knowing that a respected scholar shared my thoughts further inspired me to pursue this inquiry for over three decades, despite the lack of similar views in existing commentaries.

As I developed these ideas, the depth and potential impact of this prayer became increasingly clear to me. I shared these insights through a sermon series at our home church and in various classes, engaging in many discussions. Surprisingly, the power of Jesus' words sparked a renewed appreciation for this prayer among those who explored its truths with me. Their strong encouragement underscored the need to publish these insights, hoping to breathe new life into this ancient prayer for others.

The faith community at Oak Grove Church, MN, has been incredibly supportive, showing endless patience, kindness, and motivation to share these hopeful words. My family has also been a pillar of support; my wife and children encouraged me to integrate this work into my professional life and to heed the Spirit's promptings to delve deeper into this prayer. I am eternally grateful to them.

This book is crafted for those who feel disillusioned by the church and pained by negative experiences with other believers. It invites them to find renewed purpose and freedom through Jesus' words. However, to truly grasp the power of this prayer, we must radically alter our perceptions. I liken the Lord's Prayer to two transformative images: a spiritual blueprint and DNA.

The Lord's Prayer serves as God's spiritual blueprint for a life that honors Him. As the Creator, it's logical that Jesus would provide a plan for how we should relate to Him and live out our faith. This prayer isn't just a tool for enhancing our prayer lives; it's a comprehensive guide for living righteously in a fractured world, fully equipping God's children for a life of purpose and freedom.

Similarly, consider DNA, or Deoxyribonucleic Acid, the molecule containing genetic instructions essential for development, function, growth, and reproduction in living organisms. Composed of two long strands that twist into a double helix, DNA contains codes that dictate how organisms are built and maintained. Like biological DNA, the Lord's Prayer encompasses the spiritual genetic code that disciples of Jesus need to flourish spiritually.

This divine blueprint, passed from generation to generation, ensures spiritual vitality and resilience. Understanding and applying the spiritual DNA embedded in the Lord's Prayer is crucial for disciples to overcome worldly corruption and personal brokenness, thereby fostering healthy, vibrant growth and enabling hope and healing in a troubled world.

RE-INTRODUCING THE LORD'S PRAYER

"In her book *Mystery on the Desert*, Maria Reiche describes a series of strange lines made by the Nazea in the plains of Peru, some of them covering many square miles. For years people assumed these lines were the remnants of ancient irrigation ditches. Then in 1939, Dr. Paul Kosok of Long Island University discovered that their true meaning could only be seen from high in the air. When viewed from an airplane, these seemingly random lines are enormous drawings of birds, insects, and animals."[1]

The Lord's Prayer of Matthew 6:9-13 is one of the most dynamic pictures of God's heart in Scripture. We have some of Christ's prayers in the Scriptures, but we have only one where He explicitly taught his disciples how to pray. If we carefully understand Christ's heart, we will discover this prayer transcends all other prayers, regardless of old and new covenants, culture, and ethnic obstacles. Jesus was teaching his men about the nature of prayer in a way expressed nowhere else in Scripture. This prayer taught them about their relationship with their heavenly Father and how that truth needed to impact their lives in a broken world.

---

[1] George, Timothy. "Big Picture Faith." Christianity Today, 23 Oct. 2000.

When we see how Jesus strategically unveils the full picture of The Lord's Prayer, we will experience the same awe-inspiring thrill that Dr. Kosok experienced the first time he saw the magnificent images sketched out on the ground as viewed from the air. Once we see the big picture of His divine, eternal perspective, we will suddenly see the true power of this prayer. While there have been tremendous truths extracted by others from this passage, the predominant problem is they are often viewed in seclusion, isolated truths instead of a unified teaching.

Jesus's much broader perspective on prayer helps us appreciate the full value and impact of his teaching. My goal is to show you that this prayer can radically change our lives. Once we get an aerial view, we will see a powerful picture of what it means to live for Christ.

Over the years, many have treated it as obsolete or simply a ritualized, formulaic prayer that we quote before important events and public ceremonies. Unfortunately, we have missed the incredible depth and scope of this prayer. It is a masterpiece of kingdom life that is as relevant for us today as it was when Jesus first taught it to His disciples. For many, though, this prayer has no more significance to their spiritual worldview than Maria Reiche's strange lines in the plains of Peru that looked like irrigation ditches than the enormous drawings of various animals. Once the Lord's Prayer is seen from the high-level view of the Father, this prayer will bring us to a thrilling new perspective of life with Christ.

Consequently, the purpose of this book is not to just give another fresh and unique interpretation of the meaning and implications of the Lord's Prayer. My desire is to reveal a bigger picture that has gone relatively unnoticed. We are often so close to the text that we miss the power of context. This *prayer* is an amazing masterpiece of the Messiah. Jesus was sculpting this transcendent prayer, not just for the disciples, but for us! If we adjust our perspective to see it the way Jesus would have us see this prayer, it will transform everything we thought we knew and understood about Jesus's teaching.

Some question if this prayer should even be called the "Lord's Prayer" because the Lord never had to pray this prayer. He never would have asked for forgiveness because He was sinless. However, it certainly *is* the Lord's Prayer from the vantage point that He is the source of this prayer, and thus, it is, in every sense of the word, His prayer. Jesus is the source, the architect, and the engineer of this magnificent prayer. He is the teacher who clarified the ramifications of God's grace to those who chose to follow him. This was a source of life for His disciples, and we will find it to be one of the greatest, untapped resources that is indispensable for a God-honoring life.

The Lord's Prayer is powerful for us today, not just because Jesus is its originator but because it addresses issues that are intensely relevant to you and me. Jesus deals with things common to all believers, not things unique to any culture or ethnic group. This prayer is not about fulfilling Old Testament promises or things that only belong to the New Testament. These issues bridge how His children relate to Him, live with and for Him, and impact a fallen world.

Jesus stepped into the problem of sin, temptation, and Satan. But He also addressed the reality of God, righteousness, and His kingdom. This prayer was intended to deal with the essential struggles every person who hopes to enter in relationship with God must deal with, regardless of context. His prayer clarifies our self-worth, how we define significance, and how we experience a secure life that flourishes. This prayer scans the breadth and depth of one's entire life and the crucial issues every believer must grapple with through the scope of his or her life.

Two fundamental premises leverage my understanding of the Lord's Prayer. *First, this prayer is forged directly out of Jesus's baptism and temptation experience in Matthew 3:13-4:11.* This is not original insight; commentators have demonstrated insightful nuances between these passages for years. But there is more to the parallels than simply nuances of meaning, similar concepts, or common terminology. The parallels between the two texts are much more deeply intertwined and significant because Jesus created this prayer based on these experiences.

In this light, the temptation experience provides clarity on the more veiled components of the prayer and clarifies confusing ambiguities. It is out of His temptation we see both the humanity of Jesus and the power of God's beloved Son (Matthew 3:17). This prayer is not just a revelation from paradise through a prophet, but it is the linchpin revelation that explains God's kingdom work on earth and the expectations God has for His people. Ultimately, we see the Father's blessing validated by the Son's faithfulness; we are given a glimpse into the faithful High Priest who sympathizes with our weaknesses. We have a God who understands every struggle, temptation, and anxious experience in our journey.

The second premise, which is even more critical than the first, is that the remaining text of Matthew 6:14 through 7:27 is Jesus's exposition of His own prayer. These two chapters are not just random or segmented topics that follow the Lord's Prayer, as many suggest, but a critical exegesis by Jesus on His own prayer.

Jesus not only taught His disciples how to pray but, in a most unique and powerful display of divine wisdom, Jesus explained the significance of this prayer. Phrase by phrase, He helps His disciples grasp the full implications of every statement as it comes to bear on how they ought to live. Jesus left nothing to chance for the inductive imagination of His followers. He carefully outlines both the substance of your relationship with their heavenly Father and surgically identifies key responsibilities we all hold in the Kingdom of God as the outworking of His words.

Jesus was clearly the expert on the true meaning and application of His prayer. His intent was to outline for His men the foundational pillars of kingdom community. These truths are the non-negotiables, the sine qua non, of kingdom life. Like a modern-day church doctrinal statement that outlines the core doctrines that frame our Christian Faith, Jesus dictated the core essentials of kingdom life for His people.

From Jesus's perspective, this prayer was far too vital to leave anything to misinterpretation. He was the teacher and the exegete. Jesus knew that following Him would be a radical commitment of beliefs, values, and priorities that were unlike anything they could presently understand. It would cost them everything and require the full measure of faith to cultivate the spiritual resiliency to live out the divine requirements of kingdom life. He would leave nothing to chance.

Consequently, this prayer gives us an amazing and unique insight into the heart of Christ as He explained to His men what it really means to call God their Father. It was designed to keep their spiritual and moral compass aligned properly with their heavenly Father amid a severely damaged world.

It is vital to restate that the overflow of Chapters 6-7 is not an eclectic collection of unrelated topics that follow the Lord's Prayer but Jesus's very own exegesis of this prayer. He was not just teaching the disciples a method of praying, nor was it just another prayer among several found in the Bible. For His men to ignore the significance of this prayer would be to miss the power of God's kingdom life here on earth. The only way for these disciples to truly grasp the implications of this prayer was to see it through His eyes, to get Jesus's 30,000-foot divine perspective. Without the full picture, this would become just another prayer in a list of meaningful options.

The way we use this prayer as simply a spiritual blessing at formal events may be offensive to the heart of our Father. This prayer gives a divine worldview that can stimulate our spirit and shock our own finite, myopic blind spots. It rises above the ethnocentric clutter of cultural religion and personal pride to thrust us upon a divine vision that places God's kingdom on the front lines for His covenant community. For those wounded by institutional religion, Jesus calls to us through His prayer to consider His solution for hope and healing in a renewed relationship with your heavenly Father.

Jesus defined our relationship to Our Father, Who is in heaven, set out His kingdom priorities, and outlined behaviors that distinctly identify His disciples as His kingdom people. He will introduce His beliefs, values, priorities, behaviors, habits, and character so that His holy people actively live out His kingdom purpose.

We will also discover some answers to some rather daunting questions from the larger scope of Matthew chapters 6 and 7. What does it really mean to desire God's kingdom to come? In an affluent culture like America, how do we really translate "give us this day our daily bread" when we experience little or no need? What does it really mean to ask God not to lead us into temptation? How does a statement like, "Do not give what is holy to dogs; and do not throw pearls before swine" (Matthew 7:6, NRSV) become a powerful statement about kingdom life and not a meaningless idiomatic saying? Are the two gates in Matthew 7:13 talking about how to get saved or two ways of living? Finally, what does the ominous statement of Matthew 7:21, "Not everyone who says to me 'Lord,

Lord', will enter the kingdom of heaven" mean? Can we really lose our salvation, and what does this have to do with the Lord's Prayer? It's only in the greater context of the Lord's Prayer that we can begin to understand some of these difficult texts and clarify elusive ambiguities.

This prayer is certainly not for the weak of heart. It will take what we know of this Scripture and evoke a new responsibility and gift to us, radically changing how we live out our lives. Hidden in plain sight, one of the best-kept secrets of Scripture will become one of the most powerful tools for knowing our God and living out the life He calls us to live.

CHAPTER 1

THE LORD'S PRAYER DNA

*Why This Prayer
Changes Everything*

I was born in Calgary, Alberta, and raised under the views of the towering, 11,000-foot-high Rocky Mountains. I remember chatting with some friends who traveled to see the Alberta Rockies for a vacation. These towering sentinels guard the rugged backcountry between the western edge of Alberta and British Columbia. This was their first time seeing this part of the country. Their reaction was awesome. They had never seen anything like it in their entire lives, and for them, it was breathtaking. Certainly, they had seen pictures in magazines and travel brochures, but they had never seen the Rockies in person. They could not stop shaking their heads in disbelief. They struggled to find the words to describe these majestic wonders of creation. While I still love the beauty of this inspiring backdrop, I realized that I had become so familiar with seeing these every day growing up that they no longer took my breath away.

Familiarity breeds contempt. Contempt might seem like a strong word, but enthusiasm for anything of value is difficult to sustain. Our eagerness, even for things that truly impacted our lives, is not easily sustainable. The power of the past begins to diminish over time.

Familiarity lures us to neglect things we claim have great value. We take people for granted, like our freedoms, privileges, and opportunities. We develop an attitude of entitlement rather than thankfulness. This attitude also infects our relationship with our heavenly Father. Our spiritual priorities often diminish in the shadow of a hardening heart.

Taking things for granted is often a problem of affluence. Taking people for granted is often the result of relational neglect. Everyone has relationships, experiences, and material goods they take for granted and do not value as they once did. This is the complex reality facing us when we approach the Lord's Prayer. It is easy to have contempt because of our familiarity with the content and, in addition, we have lost the value of the prayer. Our relationship with our heavenly Father has diminished because of our delusion of self-sufficiency.

We may have experienced this if we grew up in a church. Some churches recite The Lord's Prayer repeatedly. We have rehearsed it in religious ceremonies, dedicated events, formal inaugurations, and graduations. It has become an unconscious, automatic religious routine. We have heard it in public places like sports games, school ceremonies, and government events. It is hard to get excited about something that has become a mere formality, especially when we know many people quoting it have little or no interest in Christ at all.

We have memorized and studied the Lord's Prayer. We have searched to find deeper meaning but found it hard to pull something new out of basic material. We are already familiar with the topics, but the overabundance of resources makes this prayer appear unnecessary. Our perspective has become myopic when our greatest efforts terminate on whether we should pray this prayer, word for word, to make it meaningful, or it is designed to be a model, a guide to shape our general thoughts towards our heavenly Father. We have been told it is important, but we are unsure how.

We may have thought that the Christian life would be more exciting, dramatic, and filled with miraculous moments. But those stories always seem to be someone else's journey. The Christian life can be frustrating. Even some of the milestone experiences in our own lives just may not seem to measure up to the powerful stories of others. Our inner life may feel more reflective of Solomon's lament over the emptiness and futility of life than the abundant life that Jesus offered.

It is confusing when our story is filled with trials and hardship when others seem free of conflict; we may not be desperate but certainly discouraged. Comparing our life to others or our church to other churches seems fruitless, but it can be hard to know what to focus on because everyone uses a different measure of success. It is very tempting to just forget about the church and go our own way. There is a subtle whisper deep in our hearts to think that we can do a better job of this on our own.

You may have struggled with a God you cannot see. You might have even come to the point of being disillusioned with God. You thought this divine relationship would fix things for you. Life has become so uncertain and chaotic that people question their fundamental beliefs, including God. Everything has been called into question. You have called upon God but wonder if He is listening.

Everyone wants a concierge, not another authority. God was supposed to guarantee some measure of success in life, but you do not know what that means anymore. No wonder you have become disappointed with God, the church, and other Christians. But they are not all to blame. We all struggle; this is normal, but sometimes, our frustration with others is a cover for dealing with our own struggles.

We all have internal battles that we do not want exposed to anyone; ongoing struggles of self-worth and significance. The unshakable confusion about our purpose here on earth can be unrelenting. The idea of making a difference sounds great, but that seems overwhelming. We often find ourselves discouraged and take the comments of others very personally.

Everyone tends to struggle with relationships. There are times we cannot stand to be around people, and yet what other people think carries the weight of the world with it. We are overly sensitive to people's comments, and we are not even sure how to process casual conversation. The struggle with worry and anxiety can be both exhausting and frustrating, sometimes out of control. If people understood our deepest struggles, we are certain they would abandon us.

Whether we were not given the right information or misunderstood what was taught, we may feel we are drifting away from our faith. Many are tired of going along with the crowd and want to experience genuine transformation in their life. They are tempted to think that the only way to salvage their faith is to abandon all these things that seem to do nothing, but they struggle with the guilt of making such a brash choice.

This was why we thought it was important to belong to a church family, to find some relief from all this chaos. We wanted answers to some significant questions we have carried for years. We committed to a church family and participated in the programs, but you are not sure what all that has accomplished. We live with this subtle anxiety that we have committed to a religious system, but it is not very relational. We do not know if we are the problem or if God, for some reason, does not keep His promises.

The church, however, does not appear to be in much better shape than the world. There seems to be as much tension in the church as in the culture. People have cultivated an attitude of complaining and criticism, not one of love and encouragement. Some are better experts about politics than the Bible. We get tired of performing and doing all that is expected but feeling like impostors. Sometimes, it is hard not to feel disingenuous and uncertain how to resolve it.

Everyone seems preoccupied with differences between church practices. Nobody is trying to figure out how we are to love one another well, and it feels like many have lost their way. We want guidance and wisdom, but we need someone we can really trust. Everyone needs someone to help them navigate these landmines they face in our world. Those issues have not gone away.

As magnificent and beautiful as the world appears, you know an evil lurks under the surface, permeating the fabric of everything. We want to believe in people's basic goodness, but everything seems broken, and the futility of this life is palpable at times. I can only encourage you to take another look at Jesus.

While it feels like systemic issues are making real change impossible, there is the remote possibility that a realignment to the One we ought to have been listening to in the first place suggests something different. However, changing everything around us may not actually change things for us. We sense that if we strip away all the distractions, things will be better, but ultimately, we need to take responsibility for ourselves and our walk with Christ.

Matthew described Jesus as having both wisdom and experience. He not only became human and endured the weight of living in a broken world, but He also lived his life well. He did not live and learn from his mistakes; He learned to live well by making the right choices. He navigated the same relational pitfalls and spiritual landmines that you must face every day.

Jesus does not assume that you and I can figure this out on our own. He knows exactly what we need to navigate this life and understands our weaknesses and limitations. We cannot do this perfectly like Him, but He is our best and only hope of doing more than just surviving. He will do what He promised, and He promised that we can find an abundant, rich, and full life. The one condition is that we need to listen carefully to what He says and trust He knows what He is talking about. But this may beg the question because this is exactly the problem. We feel disconnected from our Father, and we don't really know if we can trust Him.

WHY IS THE LORD'S PRAYER RELEVANT?

The Lord's Prayer was forged out of the celebration of Jesus's baptism and the crucible of His temptation. In other words, the source material for the very construction of this prayer was directly drawn from these two critical events that inaugurated Jesus's formal mission to God's people.

Most commentators recognize some connections between the Lord's Prayer and other segments of the Sermon on the Mount; most view this as a unified whole. Language, terms, and characters are woven in and out of the narrative to build a context leading up to Jesus teaching how to pray. In fact, one of the keys to the Lord's

Prayer is to realize that it is so much more than just a prayer. It was Jesus's revelation to a transformed life.

This prayer was not classroom theology. Jesus taught His men to pray in the shadow of religious duplicity of the Pharisees and Scribes. There were no helpful examples from their religious culture to facilitate meaningful prayer with their heavenly Father. Everything they would have seen and heard was very unhealthy and distasteful to God. The hypocrites prayed to impress people, not to develop a deep, abiding relationship with the God of Israel.

This prayer gave the disciples the keys to the kingdom. Jesus Himself tutored them on how to interact with their heavenly Father. He gave them hope that there was more to prayer than what had stagnated around them. They were approaching their heavenly Father, who knew exactly the struggles they would face and provided the resources to empower these disciples to honor Him in real-world challenges. Jesus's baptismal and temptation experiences exposed Him to the fundamental challenges every human will face. These struggles are deeply embedded into the fabric of reality, revealing our finiteness and weaknesses. These are not cultural challenges as much as the struggle of the human heart, common to everyone.

On the one hand, we know that Jesus was perfect and sinless. He is our High Priest: holy, innocent, undefiled, separate from sinners (Hebrews 7:26). On the other hand, He was made like His brothers in every respect so that he might become a merciful and faithful high priest (Hebrews 2:17). We do not have a high priest who is unable to sympathize with our weaknesses, but one who in every respect has been tempted as we are, yet without sin (Hebrews 4:15). He modeled how to honor the Father even under the most rigorous trials. The proof was His wilderness experience of being tempted by the devil. He was not just an example of how to live well; He was the model for His followers.

Jesus built the Lord's Prayer for His disciples, perfectly designed to help them live honoring their heavenly Father in the best of times and when facing the harshest realities. *Think of the Lord's Prayer as a direct response from Jesus to all your personal challenges.* He understands temptation and can teach you how to choose well.

One of the most critical truths Jesus demonstrated was the indispensable nature of authentic relationships, the most critical being with His heavenly Father. Nothing demonstrated this more powerfully than the Father's declaration about the nature of His relationship with His Son at His baptism: "This is my beloved Son, in whom I am well pleased" (Matthew 3:17).

Before Matthew records Jesus doing anything – before He called His disciples, preached messages, healed the sick, or did any miracles – the Father declared His love and delight in His Son. What Matthew makes noticeably clear is that God's declaration was not a celebration of successful accomplishments or outstanding achievements. This was not a recap of Jesus's legacy. It was His testimony of pure delight in His relationship with the Son before He began His mission or ministry.

The message of Jesus's baptism was the guarantee of the power of the Father's personal presence. The Father was obviously present with His Son at His baptism, evidenced by His declaration and blessing (Matthew 3:16-17). The Spirit of God was with Jesus in the wilderness. The Father sent angels to Jesus to minister to His needs at the culmination of those trials (Matthew 4:11). The Father never abandoned His Son; He was persistently present regardless of the circumstances.

Jesus fulfilled all righteousness in his baptism and chose righteousness through His temptation. Fulfilling all righteousness inferred that Jesus participated in and supported a greater plan. The Father sent His Son to accomplish the Father's will. Sending His only Son into the crucible of temptations may appear cruel and unfair. But this act was not an exception to the Father acting in righteousness; it demonstrated the essential need for righteousness.

Jesus was without human companionship in the wilderness, but He was never alone. No other factor was more important throughout these experiences than His relationship with the Father and the Holy Spirit. Nothing else would be more vital for His disciples if they were choosing to follow Jesus. The Father would never leave or forsake them. His disciples would face challenging life circumstances and the devil. The pressure to acquiesce under the weight of temptation would be enormous, but Jesus's example allowed them to see God's pathway in very dark situations. His example and presence helped them through those exact issues.

Since everyone is part of the human race, we all face the same challenges, temptations, and trials. Jesus was not addressing cultural crises; He was addressing divine needs and spiritual provisions. Jesus showed how foundational these components are, not just for the disciples but for every disciple that will follow Christ through faith. Jesus mentored His men to understand the profound privilege they had to be in a relationship with the God of the universe.

This was the foundation of a transformed life. While many of us dream about what we want to do when we grow up, Christ is concerned about what we become when we follow Him.

THE EXAMPLE OF JESUS

Jesus refused to define right and wrong based only on His personal needs or self-interest. Jesus fasted forty days and nights. The devil tempted Jesus to turn stones into bread and said that no one would find fault with action taken to meet such a critical need. Instead, Jesus gave a history lesson to highlight God's dealings with Israel in the wilderness. He let them go hungry to test what was in their heart and gave them manna to provide for them. They needed to learn that "man does not live by bread alone, but every word from the mouth of God" (Deuteronomy 8:3). Israel's most basic need for food could not be allowed to take precedence over the Father's will.

Jesus embedded this fundamental principle deep into the fabric of this prayer so His men would embrace the Father first, even before personal need. The very nature of this experience would be profoundly relevant for these ordinary men as they sought to follow Jesus. Some of the greatest failures and successes in Biblical history revolve around the basic needs of life.

Adam and Eve sinned over a piece of fruit. Israel was tested when God let them go hungry in the wilderness. Israel forgot God when they had an abundance of basic resources. Samuel anointed Saul as king over a meal. Jesus's first temptation revolved around food. One of the most important ordinances of the church, the Lord's Supper, was established around a traditional meal. As anticlimactic as it may seem, Jesus taught His men to ask for the Father's provision for daily bread at the very heart of the Lord's Prayer. Jesus knew that basic needs were a strategic leverage point for spiritual success or failure in the life of God's people.

It is easy to make excuses or blame others for our personal failures. Often, our struggles are self-imposed neglect of our relationship with our heavenly Father. Often, there is no one else to blame. Many, like Israel, have become too enamored by their own self-importance and the distractions in the world. We abandon our relationship with God to pursue selfish things. Nothing could be more relevant to broken human beings attempting to live with Jesus.

My teen years were exactly this struggle. I spent too much time comparing my self-worth with a misguided perception that everyone else had their life put together. I exhausted myself, competing for significance. I built my security around the acceptance of others rather than my relationship with Christ. I was a prisoner of my own devices, cloaked under a veil of humility but succumbing to a vicious self-centeredness.

The second temptation Jesus faced was regarding power. Satan provoked Jesus to prove His authority as the Son of God by throwing Himself off the temple. The inherent danger of power is the corruptive nature of pride. Jesus rightly rebuked Satan by pointing out that testing "the LORD your God" was the pinnacle of arrogance (Matthew 4:5-7).

Jesus's third temptation proposed the idea that the end justifies the means. The devil tempted Jesus to secure all the kingdoms of the world without going to the cross. This was the very reason for Jesus's incarnation and mission, to bring about the redemption of fallen humanity! If there was a means to accomplish this without succumbing to the suffering of the cross, it would have seemed like a divine opportunity.

The offer to attain His divine purpose and avoid the cross appeared to be a solution. No principle could be more significant for Christ's disciples than understanding that God was not only concerned about the end results but also the means of getting there. Making choices that align with the Father's will are the only ones that reflect true righteousness. Not only are the results important, but also the pathway to get there. Both must reflect the Father's will and righteousness.

The most difficult aspect of human choice is the ability to tell right from wrong. Human morality has fluctuated from legalism to simply doing what is right in one's own eyes. The fluidity of morality has not been accidental. The devil undermined God's objective authority with Adam and Eve. He attempted to do this with Jesus in the wilderness, and he will keep on attacking God's people in this manner, too.

The temptation to think we can become our own authority has been the ongoing struggle of God's people. Jesus demonstrated that God's standard of righteousness is far more important than proving He could deal with temptations on His own. Doing what was right in our own eyes always involves taking the risk that what makes sense to us is what God desires. Sometimes, they may end up being the same choice. This was not just for the disciples; it was significant for all of God's people.

Jesus experienced the full gamut of human triumph and tragedy. In His baptism, He was affirmed by the highest authority of the Father. It was done in a public context, and everything about it was exactly right. The fact that the Spirit of God drove Jesus into this deserted wilderness for the purpose of being tempted by the devil would appear, on every human level, to be an act of betrayal. In one moment, Jesus was celebrated and, on the other hand, placed in harm's way! Jesus understood the stark reality that life can be cruel and unfair. All of this unfolded according to the Father's purpose and righteousness. Jesus understood the good and the bad things of life.

While there is an obvious uniqueness to the Father's relationship with His one and only Son, this is the same attitude that the Father desires for all His children. When you came to faith in Christ, the Father celebrated you as a beloved son or daughter. He removed you from judgment, He forgave your sin, He gave you His

Son's righteousness and adopted you into His family. In that divine moment, He fully accepted you as family, and you now belong to Him. You are His beloved child in whom He takes great delight.

Before you even started your walk with God, before you learned about your spiritual responsibilities, or before you served, discovered your gifts, participated in a small group, or followed Jesus on a mission, the Father delighted in you. This unmitigated delight will not change regardless of how bumpy the road is ahead. His love and affection are never contingent on our performance. His familiarity with you will never breed contempt. Your heavenly Father will never become bored or indifferent in His love and commitment to you. His pleasure is not dependent on what you do; it is dependent on what Christ did for you!

Why is the Lord's Prayer Relevant Today?

My kids are social media experts, not me. They were bred on these platforms, but social media is a foreign language to me. Like most parents, I often ask my kids for help with these things. When I need to learn how to use a platform, I do not ask them how to do it; I ask them to *show* me how to do it!

The Lord's Prayer is a gift from the Father through His Son to show us a spiritual blueprint for a God-honoring life. Jesus taught the essentials for a dynamic relationship with the Father. He also taught the Father's expectations to honor Him and serve Him well. Jesus is our example, mentor, and model. Since He set our standard, He becomes the paradigm. Since God does not change, that same relationship is viable for us as much as it was for His disciples.

Responsibilities are connected to relationships. One of the greatest struggles for God's people is to treat their Father in heaven as a real person instead of a religious concept. Jesus did not just teach the Father's priorities, but He showed how to live them out in a vital relationship with Him. Jesus modeled every aspect of His relationship to the Father, the responsibility to obey His will, and the indispensable nature of both to shape lives in a broken world. Relationship with God never becomes obsolete. Jesus's example set during His life on earth is the perfect model for our lives as well.

When the disciples began following Jesus, they were stepping into something completely new. They had no resume to qualify them for following Christ and engaging His mission. The disciples had much to learn. Jesus was their advocate, teaching them and walking with them through relational pitfalls and spiritual land-mines.

You and I find ourselves in the same scenario as Jesus's disci-ples. Nothing in our life experience qualifies us for a relationship with the Father, but following Jesus is the requirement for life with the Father! Jesus has given you and me the same opportunity.

This is what makes the Lord's Prayer far more than just a prayer to recite in a service. This prayer reflects the riches of His grace to help us navigate dangers in this world and live a Spirit-empowered life that honors God. There is nothing lacking in this prayer. In many ways, it is Jesus's guarantee to sufficiently help us fulfill ex-actly what the Father requires.

GOD AS OUR HEAVENLY FATHER

"What comes to your mind when you think about God is the most important thing about you."[2] If our thoughts about God are dis-torted, our relationship with God will suffer. Jesus gave us the most powerful picture we need to have when we think about God: He is our heavenly Father.

Unlike human fathers, He has none of the failings or short-comings that burdened our earthly fathers. He is merciful, gra-

---

[2] A.W. Tozer. *The Knowledge of the Holy.* General Press, 2019.

cious, long-suffering, and abounding in goodness and truth. He extends compassion, and He forgives. Our heavenly Father understands this world far better than we do. What is lacking from our earthly parents, our heavenly Father provides.

This is not the picture that many people have about God. Many Christians do not see God as a loving Father who delights in them. Some see Him as a religious taskmaster, demanding obedience and conformity. Others see God as a judge, always watching to catch them failing. Some see God as an irritated dad who yells to control his kids and constantly expresses his disappointment. These images do not foster a healthy picture of our heavenly Father. The absence of trust, love, and kindness does not transfer to the idea that God delights in us. More importantly, these negative thoughts do not accurately represent God's character.

The privilege of calling God "Father" also defines our new identity as His children. The disciples no longer defined themselves as fishermen or tax collectors. They are children of God serving their Father's interests by following His Son. What their Father said was true about them, but they needed to reshape their mindset in order to transcend any negative opinions of family, friends, and even their own thoughts! This new identity gave them freedom regarding their true value and worth as His children. But since God cares so much for His children, we must resolve why so many dreadful things happen to us. Why does God allow such hard things to happen to His children?

We all live in a world of evil. The news is filled with unimaginable events recently—the war in Ukraine, the invasion of Hamas into Israel, and the tensions with North Korea. On the home front here in America, we battle the horrific issues of child sex slavery and ethnic conflicts. The economy is struggling, and the cost of living is rising. There are daily news bulletins of shootings. This world is struggling because awful things happen. This evil flies in the face of our heavenly Father, and it challenges you and me to resolve a good God in a suffering world. Seeing all these bad things around us is overwhelming, but it is even more troubling to experience them when they happen to us.

We have all experienced bad things. Life is inundated with hardship, trials, and evil. We have suffered isolation, abuse, and injustice in various degrees of severity. Sometimes, deliberately or unintentionally, family members are the source of these trials, undermining our self-worth and significance. Friends say unkind things out of their insecurity. Those who claim to love us betray us when we are most vulnerable. The trauma of these wounds feels like an inescapable prison. All of these things could make us wonder if God cares because we assume He would protect His children from bad stuff. It raises the question of how we think about our relationship with our heavenly Father and our expectations of Him as we live in this broken world.

Jesus taught that our heavenly Father is holy and perfect in character and purpose. He has never been corrupted by evil on earth. For us, evil is an unconquerable enemy that afflicts humanity and all creation with futility, suffering, and death. The curse that God imposed on creation and sinful humanity holds sin at bay and exposes the vanity of the human heart to find worth, significance, and security apart from a genuine relationship with our Creator. This reality cannot be ignored or dismissed. Since the devil launched a full-on attack against Jesus, he will be just as aggressive against His followers.

If God is holy and good, then it might seem He is not doing a particularly good job dealing with evil. God is not the author of evil, nor does He tempt us with evil (James 1:12-15). Yet the Spirit of God intentionally led Jesus into the wilderness for the purpose of being tempted by the devil, which appears to contradict both God's character and the teaching of Scripture. God created humanity with the freedom to choose; the first human couple decided to ignore God, make their own choices, and open the door to pervasive suffering, struggle, conflict, and hardships. These afflictions were the collateral damage of separating from Him.

God's response was to launch an all-out rescue mission, sending His only Son to reclaim a lost humanity. The cost of this rescue was far more brutal and unimaginable than anyone could imagine; it was the sacrifice of His Son. God was willing to sacrifice what was most precious to Himself to meet the deepest need of humanity. If we grasp that God loved humanity this much when everyone was His enemy, we can see how much He delights to give to His children all that we need!

Only the Son of our heavenly Father can provide answers for you. The solution is not religion or philosophy – and certainly not surfing the web! Only He can deal with our separation from the Father. He alone can answer the deep problems from the sinful scar on His image within you. This is not solved by believing in the idea of Jesus but rather by discovering the power of His personal presence dwelling in you!

Finally, their Father calls Jesus's disciples to a life shaped by divine purpose. Jesus came to fulfill the Father's purpose to redeem lost humanity and set us free from the power of sin and death. Jesus called His disciples to a relationship with Him to equip them to carry out the Father's kingdom work here on earth as God planned it in heaven.

This kingdom of heaven is to be the heartbeat of His children. This is to be our highest priority and value. God's kingdom was inaugurated by Jesus, continued by His disciples, and will be fulfilled in the future according to the Father's will. Jesus told His disciples that they were to seek first the Father's kingdom and His righteousness. This gave their lives a divine purpose greater than the distractions of life.

The Lord's Prayer is Christ's personal design to transform your life. Jesus will teach you the Father's expectations for how you are to live and personally show you how to understand this prayer from His perspective so that it transforms your life.

The Christian life is not mysticism or blind faith. Jesus offered something enormously powerful to help you navigate life in a way that honors your heavenly Father. That resource has been hidden in plain sight due to its frequent superficial and shallow usage. The riches of His grace are inseparable from the power of His personal presence. His wisdom is captured by the prayer that He used to teach us how to avail ourselves of His deep grace.

PRINCIPLES ABOUT GOD'S SPIRITUAL BLUEPRINT

1. The Lord's Prayer was created out of Jesus's baptism and temptation experiences. Jesus speaks out of divine revelation and personal experience in dealing with the very things we must face in life.

   - What did you learn about Jesus' relationship with His Father in His baptism?
   - What do you observe as Jesus faced His temptations and how He responded?
   - What temptations in your own life help you connect with Jesus' temptations?

2. The Lord's Prayer was designed as a spiritual blueprint to help the disciples recognize and overcome the spiritual landmines in life, specifically dealing with evil in the world and how it impacts one's life.

   - How would you explain Jesus' blueprint?
   - Which parts of this blueprint can you relate to your own experiences?
   - Which aspects of this blueprint are most disturbing to you? Why?

3. The Lord's Prayer helps disciples navigate the confusing and sometimes complicated world of relationships, especially when one has been hurt or damaged by the actions of others.

   - What are the most challenging relationships you are facing in your life? How would you describe your response to these people?
   - What principles in this prayer would impact how you are relating to these people?

- What truths do you need to take more seriously?

4. The Lord's Prayer emphasizes that His disciples have a relationship with the most powerful person in the universe, whom we have the privilege to call Father.

  - How would you describe your present relationship with your Heavenly Father?
  - What have you learned that will help you grow in your relationship with your Father?
  - What next step do you need to take to grow in His grace?

PRAYER

Lord, help me to see Your fingerprints on every aspect of my life journey, regardless if my circumstances appear good or bad. Give me the perspective that You have called me to live a godly life in a broken world, damaged and fragmented by sin and evil. Help me see Your goodness and mercy in the hardest moments of life. Give me understanding of Your grace and kindness when everything is going well.

Constantly remind me that You work all things together for good to those who love You. You have a purpose for every event and circumstance for my good. You celebrate me as Your child and continue to refine my character to the image of Your Son. May I continually discover the satisfaction of Your grace and rejoice in the power of Your personal presence. In Christ's strong name, Amen.

CHAPTER 2

OUR FATHER: IT'S PERSONAL

Getting Real About Your Connection with God

"Our Father, who [is] in the heavens, hallowed by Your name…"

Matthew 6:9, LSV

"For if you forgive others their trespasses, your heavenly Father will also forgive you, but if you do not forgive others their trespasses, neither will your Father forgive your trespasses. And when you fast, do not look gloomy like the hypocrites, for they disfigure their faces that their fasting may be seen by others. Truly, I say to you, they have received their reward. But when you fast, anoint your head and wash your face, that your fasting may not be seen by others but by your Father who is in secret. And your Father who sees in secret will reward you."

Matthew 6:14-18

One of the challenges of being in a family is maintaining healthy relationships. Some families know the blessing of rich, deep, loving relationships that nurture each other.

Siblings learn respect, generosity, teamwork, and character. However, some families are very dysfunctional, so normal life skills become distorted, and people learn survival techniques rather than life skills. Relationships are hard because of abusive, controlling, and manipulative home environments.

Parents set the family's values and culture. While no family is perfect, and every child will have something they need to forgive their parents for, parents have a huge impact on their children's personal and spiritual health. While both parents are critical to children's development, the element most relevant to the Lord's Prayer is that of the Father.

One of the last memorial services I did for a family was for a faithful servant of the Lord, a husband and father who others respected and loved. Time was provided in the service to allow individuals to share stories about their connection with this gentleman. While it is impossible to capture a person's life in one service, family and friends alike shared the most outstanding characteristics that impacted them because of their relationship to this person.

Everyone shared fun experiences, challenging events, and a list of character traits. Regardless of the stories, most people would usually make some statement, as is often done memorializing a person's life, highlighting the one or two things they will always remember that stand above every other memory. It did not mean there were not numerous other things that could be said about him, but these were the characteristics that stood above the rest.

The Lord's Prayer was far too important for Jesus to allow the disciples, or anyone for that matter, to misunderstand, misinterpret, or communicate the wrong picture of their heavenly Father. The volume of truth Jesus could have shared about the nature and character of our heavenly Father would have been astronomically overwhelming. Jesus chose to be very selective about the key qualities that He knew would be the most critical for His people to have crystal clear in their mind when they thought about this particular relationship.

Jesus expounded on three characteristics that defined the disciples' relationship with God: He is our Father, He is transcendent, and He is holy; more specifically, His name is holy. The first two elements can be expounded on from the prayer itself. Jesus's commentary in the following verses best understands the nature of being a Father and being holy.

GOD IS OUR HEAVENLY FATHER.

The God of Israel was their Father. By addressing God as Father, Jesus taught that God is personal. God created us to be in relationship with Him. Since humanity was created in His image, everyone has the capacity for relationship, not just with other humans, but with God Himself. This designation of "Father" also indicates God wants to be close to His children. This was not just about friendship but family. A Father's delight in His family is unique and powerful. Jesus taught about the nature of relationship to God as Father, declaring God's desire to be in close proximity to His children, to experience life with them as their Father.

Children (especially young children) thrive on the personal presence of their father. In a healthy father-child relationship, the father desires to be involved in his children's life experiences. Developing a healthy sense of self-worth, significance, and security are cultivated by a father who exudes love, compassion, forgiveness, and mercy (among a host of other character qualities) to his young children.

Jesus often used young children to communicate the nature of God's kingdom. In Matthew 18, Jesus used the simple faith of little children to define how adults may enter the kingdom of heaven. In Matthew 19:13-14, Jesus used little children again to describe the true nature of being in the Father's kingdom. The best pictures clarifying what it means to belong to God's kingdom are the simple faith and trust of children.

The most powerful truth about the disciples' relationship to their heavenly Father is that He always viewed them, even grown men, like His young children who needed Him to be involved in their life experiences. He committed to taking them by the hand and leading them through every challenge and circumstance.

This was the picture Jesus was imprinting into his disciples' minds. When young children have a strong relationship with their father, he is their hero, and there is no one like their dad. They consider their dad to be the best dad in the world and adore him because they think he is unique. He is powerful and kind. He helps children form identity, significance, and security.

OUR FATHER IS TRANSCENDENT

Our Father dwells in the heavens. Birds were created to fly in the heavens, which are equal to the atmosphere of the earth (Genesis 1:20). The stars dwell in the night heavens (Isaiah 13:10), which defines another aspect of heaven with greater breadth and scope. Paul spoke about the third heaven, which he called paradise, where he met God in an unusual manner (2 Corinthians 12:2-4). The term used here in this prayer, heavens, is plural.

Our heavenly Father is transcendent above all heavens. He is the creator of everything, the architect, the designer, and the engineer of everything that exists, both visible and invisible. His fingerprints are on everything, including our existence. Nowhere is the captured more vividly than with Psalmist:

"Where can I go from Your Spirit? Or where can I flee from Your presence? If I ascend into heaven, You *are* there; If I make my bed in hell, behold, You are *there. If* I take the wings of the morning, *and* dwell in the uttermost parts of the sea, Even there Your hand shall lead me, and Your right hand shall hold me."

Psalm 139:7-10, NKJV

When Adam and Eve sinned, they fled from God because of fear and shame. The Psalmist takes comfort in the fact that God cares enough for him that there is nowhere he could ever go in all of creation that God would not be consciously present. The Lord is his comfort, guide, and provider. He would never be truly alone.

OUR FATHER IS HOLY

Jesus taught the disciples that God is holy. The idea of the word "hallowed" is to make something holy or to sanctify. To be holy is to be set apart. God is holy because it is His nature. He does not need anyone's input to become holy; He is utterly unique from everyone and everything. But God expects His children to treat Him as holy. In practical terms, a child wants nothing more from their dad than for him to be proud of them. They live for his praise and encouragement. There is no better picture of what it means for God's children to treat Him as holy than a young child's great delight to please their father. God's desire for His children is for us to live to reflect the character of their Dad.

Holiness has a moral component. Holiness carries the idea of purity. Negatively, this means living untainted by the corruption that infects the world and free from the toxic element of evil. Sin is the prevailing element holding humanity captive. Holiness is the spiritual and moral compass grounded in the character of God.

For Israel, God was merciful, gracious, slow to anger, and abundant in steadfast love. He was faithful and forgiving. But godliness was obedience to the Law. Israel did not have the right to define right and wrong for themselves. They were obligated to submit to their Creator and allow Him to reveal exactly what He expected from His people.

Jesus outlined godly character in the Beatitudes. He taught that characteristics that honor the Father are meekness, mercy, and seeking righteousness with a pure heart. The New Testament outlines the fruit of the Spirit as holiness or godliness. There are numerous ways we can explore how disciples should live if they seek to honor their heavenly Father and respect His holy name.

OUR FATHER FORGIVES

At this moment in the text, Matthew directs us to Jesus's commentary in Matthew 6:14-18 on what it means to address God as Father and to respect His holiness. He records Jesus's words explaining two critical qualities that will always be true if disciples truly honor their heavenly Father and esteem His holiness. The first quality Jesus wants them to keep foremost in their minds when they think about God as their Father is forgiveness. The second was a posture they were to have that demonstrated their reverence for His holiness – humility.

Our first responsibility is to understand the nature of forgiveness:

> "For if you forgive others their trespasses, your heavenly Father will also forgive you, but if you do not forgive others their trespasses, neither will your Father forgive your trespasses. "And when you fast, do not look gloomy like the hypocrites, for they disfigure their faces that their fasting may be seen by others. Truly, I say to you, they have received their reward. But when you fast, anoint your head and wash your face, that your fasting may not be seen

by others but by your Father who is in secret. And your Father who sees in secret will reward you.

Matthew 6:14-18

Four times in these five verses, Jesus uses the word "Father." He deliberately overemphasized the term "Father" in these verses to connect them to His opening address in His prayer. His purpose was to imprint on their minds how they were to think about their heavenly Father when they prayed. In contrast, the term "Father" is used only four times through the following forty-four verses to conclude chapter seven! Jesus specifically connects the opening address to these five verses but hooks this concept of God being Father to the rest of His explanation to reveal that this whole section was His commentary on the very prayer He taught His disciples.

If the disciples were going to follow Jesus and navigate the challenges of His mission in a sinful world, one of the most critical truths Jesus wanted to keep at the forefront in their minds was that God was a forgiving Father. The basis of forgiveness is God's forgiveness towards us. To call God our Father required Him who is holy, to forgive those who are sinful. But to live well in His family and in fellowship with the Father also placed an expectation on the disciples to follow their Father's example by forgiving others.

Nowhere is the power of this seen more clearly than in Matthew 18:21-35:

> "Then Peter came up and said to him, "Lord, how often will my brother sin against me, and I forgive him? As many as seven times?" Jesus said to him, "I do not say to you seven times, but seventy-seven times. "Therefore, the kingdom of heaven may be compared to a king who wished to settle accounts with his servants. When he began to settle, one was brought to him who owed him ten thousand talents. And since he could

not pay, his master ordered him to be sold, with his wife and children and all that he had, and payment to be made. So the servant fell on his knees, imploring him, 'Have patience with me, and I will pay you everything.' And out of pity for him, the master of that servant released him and forgave him the debt. But when that same servant went out, he found one of his fellow servants who owed him a hundred denarii and seizing him, he began to choke him, saying, 'Pay what you owe.' So his fellow servant fell down and pleaded with him, 'Have patience with me, and I will pay you.' He refused and went and put him in prison until he could pay the debt. When his fellow servants saw what had taken place, they were greatly distressed, and they went and reported to their master all that had taken place. Then his master summoned him and said to him, 'You wicked servant! I forgave you all that debt because you pleaded with me. And should not you have had mercy on your fellow servant, as I had mercy on you?' And in anger his master delivered him to the jailers, until he should pay all his debt. So also my heavenly Father will do to every one of you if you do not forgive your brother from your heart."

It would be impossible for the disciples to forgive others if they did not understand or value the Father's forgiveness. This text deals with the issue of forgiveness in black-and-white terms. Experiencing the kindness of the Father's forgiveness but refusing to forgive others is inconsistent with His mercy and is met with the master's displeasure. The master labels him as wicked and hands him over to the torturers until he pays all his debt. Unforgiveness brings about a harsh response by subjecting the unmerciful servant to a prison of torture. Clearly, fellowship with the Father is contingent on forgiving others.

If anything is a litmus test for the claim to know God, this is placed high on the list by Jesus.

The servant's attack on his fellow servant is mind-boggling. Assaulting and threatening his fellow servant, culminating in throwing him in prison, is incomprehensible. This trauma is exacerbated by the complete lack of appreciation for the mercy shown by the master. His actions are tragic.

Many Christians have left the church because of the damage done by those who claim to know Christ's forgiveness but deliberately and carelessly wound others by imposing their own selfish desires. Spiritual bullies are an affliction that has damaged many. Asking victims of such tormentors to forgive is not just a daunting and difficult request; it may feel impossible.

Two observations of this narrative are particularly relevant to the issue of forgiving others. First, forgiveness does not give permission for anyone to keep on acting badly. The servant's actions towards his fellow servant are repulsive. He did not value the master's forgiveness. Refusing to forgive others after being forgiven violates the kindness of the master. Our heavenly Father has forgiven all of us a debt we can never pay. He desires us to extend the same kindness and grace to our fellow believers.

Secondly, the master intervened by removing the individual from the community and imprisoning him until he paid the sum of his debt. Intervention is often necessary to keep individuals from continuing to sin against others. This does not question whether the master's forgiveness was genuine, but it reveals the servant's hardness of heart to exploit forgiveness for his own purpose. Jesus explained these offenses do not go unnoticed by the Father.

That being said, there is a dark side to forgiveness. Sorting through events that inevitably demand forgiveness is often confusing. Understanding motives, distinctions between forgiving and reconciling, and discerning if forgiveness is a process or a choice complicate how we heal, forgive, and reconcile.

Some people try to control and manipulate others by demanding that others, if they are Christians, must forgive the offender. Wilco De Vries makes a sad observation about the abuse of forgiveness:

> "Forgiveness is the heartbeat of salvation history and the virtue that should mark the followers of Jesus. But those who seek to control and manipulate others can twist even the very heart of the gospel for their perverted ends. A friend of mine experienced this. She endured a hellish childhood and abuse by several family members, including her father. No one in her life intervened or spoke up. As an adult, she finally gathered the courage to confront her abusers, who misused Scriptures and twisted theology to excuse their actions and demand her silence."[3]

When offenders demand others to forgive them "because this is the responsibility of every Christian," it immediately becomes manipulation. When someone humbly seeks forgiveness by repenting of their sin, there is a genuine desire to reconcile. One is an act of exploitation, while the other seeks restoration.

The other dark side of forgiveness is manipulation by those offended. We can never overstate the emotional and spiritual suffering from betrayal. An intense internal struggle often clouds the pathway to personal healing and freedom. But Jesus's words, "Forgive us our debts as we forgive our debtors," sets the standard for

---

3 Wilco De Vries. "Abuse Victims and the Danger of Forced Forgiveness." *Christianity Today*, April 2023, www.christianitytoday.com/2023/04/abuse-victims-danger-of-forced-forgiveness/.

his disciples and must be reconciled and included in our journey no matter how painful.

Sometimes, circumstances are so overwhelming that the one sinned against feels they cannot forgive and instead chooses a different trajectory to find justice and healing. The temptation is to set aside forgiveness and skip to avoidance, survival, justice, and sometimes revenge. The problem, however, is that true healing can never exclude forgiveness. The issue to be resolved is when and where forgiveness must insert itself in this journey to experience healing and freedom.

Forgiveness is inseparably rooted in our love for God. In Luke 7, Simon the Pharisee hosted a dinner that Jesus attended. The dinner was interrupted by a woman who came in weeping. She poured perfume on Jesus' feet and washed them. Simon was indignant with the woman who intruded and with Jesus for not realizing this woman was a sinner.

Jesus challenged Simon with a brief parable about a moneylender who forgave the debt of two men, one who owed a huge debt and the other a much smaller amount (Luke 7:40-43). The key question: which one loved the moneylender more? Simon supposed that it was the one who owed the greater debt. The truth Jesus was teaching was simple: the one who is forgiven much, loves much. The one who is forgiven little, loves little (v. 47).

Our love for God is directly correlated to the degree in which we understand the significance of God's forgiveness toward us. The same universal principle applies to the Lord's Prayer. To the extent to which the disciples grasped the full measure of His love demonstrated by His forgiveness, they had an equal capacity to forgive others. If they had obstacles in their life that kept them from experiencing and valuing His love and forgiveness, they would struggle with demonstrating this kind of love to others. In other words, their unwillingness to forgive reflected a lack of understanding of God's love and His forgiveness in their life.

The way we treat others reflects how we honor our heavenly Father. Forgiving others honors Him. Grounded in the gospel, God's forgiveness is the basis for our capacity to forgive. Relationship with God should bring about transformation to be more like Christ. But living in a broken world is not that simple. The reality is that Christians struggle with forgiving others, just like we struggle with being holy, compassionate, and kind and reflecting other spiritual fruits. Believers are called to live above the selfishness of the flesh. But these expectations also contribute to our disillusionment when Christians transgress against us. We say we forgive but often harbor resentments; we claim to forgive but never really reconcile; we know we are to release people of wrongdoing, but we often remain irritated and hold grudges.

I have seen individuals leave a church family, all the while claiming to forgive someone, but they won't stay part of that faith community due to unresolved resentment towards someone who hurt them. The struggle over a lack of justice is a *real* struggle. The contingency in Matthew 6:14-15 is not about how we become a child of God but how God's children treat each other. While forgiveness may not be the characteristic that we would pick as most important in our relationship with our heavenly Father, this is the one characteristic that Jesus brought to the forefront and sets as critically important in this relationship! The power of forgiveness validates our self-worth as children of God elevates

Equal to this attribute, the second part of Jesus's interpretation is focused on the character of humility as a direct response to His holiness.

OUR FATHER IS HOLY

"And when you fast, do not look gloomy like the hypocrites, for they disfigure their faces that their fasting may be seen by others. Truly, I say to you, they have received their reward. But when you fast, anoint your head and wash your face, that your fasting may not be seen by others but by your Father who is in secret. And your Father who sees in secret will reward you."

Matthew 6:16-18

One of the biggest lessons I have learned about humility was playing in a golf tournament as a teenager. I was a very insecure kid and placed too much of my self-worth on performance. I was on the last hole of a public tournament and in no position to win. My second shot on the hole went into the left rough that was a buffer between the fairway and a pond. I looked for five minutes but could not find the ball. I started to panic in spite of the fact I was completely out of the competition.

I happened to have another golf ball in my pocket and pulled it out, reached down like I was checking for something that looked like a ball in the long grass, dropped it, and pretended I had found my original ball. I was panicking about losing my original ball and struggling with my actions. I hesitated way too long to hit my next shot; I knew it was wrong. One of the other golfers made his way down the fairway and over to my spot before I got around to hitting my next shot.

He was very kind but promptly suggested that the others in our foursome knew I had not found my ball and that if I hit the ball that I just dropped, they could have had me disqualified from the tournament. He suggested I go back to where I hit my second shot and finish the hole according to the rules. I was humiliated by my lack of integrity and choice to try and save my self-worth by cheating. In fact, the very opposite occurred. I lost more self-respect by trying to cheat! I went back, hit the ball from where my drive landed, finished the hole, and left. I was too embarrassed to stick around after my complete lack of judgment. If I had learned humility rather than waiting to humiliate myself, it would have been a very different outcome.

The second characteristic of the Father is He is holy. Jesus's exposition in Matthew 6:16-18 shows that humility is the defining response to His holiness. Humility before a Father who is holy is not only the appropriate posture but an indispensable attitude. What appears unusual is that Jesus communicated the concept of humility through the discipline of fasting.

Fasting is mentioned only eight times in Matthew. It was first mentioned when Jesus fasted in the wilderness. He was not commanded to do it. The language of the text indicates Jesus chose to fast. He did not simply go hungry because there was no food. He chose to fast for a purpose. From a human perspective, this appears foolish. This choice would be detrimental to His own well-being and make him more vulnerable to the environment and to the devil. His fasting experience was His act of humility towards His Father and the best evidence of why He uses this practice to teach His men about humility.

In these three verses, Jesus speaks about fasting four times. Jesus assumed the disciples would fast but did not command it as a practice. This avoids the dilemma of turning it into a duty to be performed rather than a heart response to a relationship with the Father. Fasting was a posture of humility for the purpose of seeking God, and, as Jesus taught, the Father would reward them for seeking Him. If the disciples wanted to understand how to humble themselves before their Father who is holy, fasting was the practice and discipline they were to embrace.

In Matthew 6:16, Jesus warned His disciples of the hypocrites who practiced fasting to be seen by others: "Do not look gloomy" like the hypocrites, and do not disfigure your faces so men may see them. In this context, fasting would appear to be an act of repentance from sin. Religious hypocrites were normal for the times and, by their very nature, were displeasing to God (Matthew 6:1-7). The disciples were not to follow them.

Hypocrites exploited a religious practice to impress others rather than seek after God. Jesus exhorted His men that fasting in secret before their Father would be rewarded. Inevitably, the Father is after our desire for Him, not our discipline. When faced with God's holiness, fasting is a picture of repentance. It is a call to return to God and find forgiveness so that God can restore His people. It can be practiced by an individual or a corporate group (Exodus 34:28; Daniel 9:3; Jonah 3:5-10).

One of the most powerful statements in the Old Testament is David's declaration in Psalm 35:13, KJV, "I humbled my soul with fasting." When faced with God's righteous judgment, fasting was David's posture of humble repentance. It was a call to return to God and find forgiveness to restore fellowship with Him. Fasting was always a means to an end, not an end in and of itself. Fasting is humility before a holy God and an appeal before a heavenly Father.

Fasting, especially when done in sackcloth and ashes, demonstrated repentance over sin, despair over a crisis, or an urgent appeal before God. (Nehemiah 1:3-4; 9:1-2; Esther 4:3; Psalm 35:13; 69:9-10; 109:22-26). Fasting openly lays bare the soul before God in all its vulnerability and pleads for His response. In both the Old and New Testaments, the very nature of fasting is humility before God. No passage better captures the heart of fasting than Joel 2:12-13:

"Yet even now," declares the LORD, "Return to Me with all your heart, And with fasting, weeping, and mourning; And tear your heart and not *merely* your garments." Now return to the LORD your God, For He is gracious and compassionate, Slow to anger, abounding in mercy And relenting of catastrophe."

Joel 2:12-13, NASB

Our concept of fasting is quite different. We fast for the purpose of de-toxifying our bodies from harmful additives in our food. We fast for the purpose of weight loss and strength training. Fasting has various applications for the purpose of dealing with our addictions to technology and social media, among other things. Fasting as a means of humbly seeking the Lord is not a common conviction, even among Christians. But divesting ourselves of fundamental needs to be completely transparent before the Lord could not provide a more powerful picture of humility. Being utterly vulnerable before a holy God captures the heart and attitude of humility.

Jesus's critique of the hypocritical religious system of the Pharisees and Scribes mirrors the Lord's appeal communicated by the prophet Joel. God's people had a desperate need to return to Him with all their hearts, even if they did not see it themselves. Their foremost safety net was their heavenly Father, who was eager to forgive them despite this deeply ingrained hypocrisy. His holiness shines the light on their sin and exposes their spiritual and moral need. His forgiveness restores and heals.

While forgiveness and holiness are distinct qualities, they were inseparable from a viable and healthy relationship with their heavenly Father. If the disciples did not believe the Father's desire to forgive, they would never find humility. If they failed to grasp humility before a holy God, they would struggle with forgiveness.

The attitude of the heart that God always promises a reward is humility (James 4:10; 1 Peter 5:6). Jesus explained to his disciples that fasting would be rewarded by their heavenly Father; He rewards those who fast because it is a physical expression of a humble heart. God rewards humility.

Without humility and a deep conviction in the Father's faithfulness to forgive, serving Christ according to His calling will also be impossible. We will face enormous challenges, most stemming from conflict either with others or with ourselves. People will give hundreds of reasons to give up and quit ministry, but God provides only one reason to stay in the ministry: His Son. One of the greatest struggles of believers is feelings of being unworthy or insignificant and attempting to use ministry to shore up these insecurities. Conversely, one of the greatest temptations is developing a god-complex where self-confidence replaces humility.

Words fail to describe how significant this one relationship is for everyone. This fellowship with a holy God who is also their heavenly Father who forgives would be essential to keep the disciples from falling back into the hypocrisy of the religious culture. They would become the new community, paving the way for a revitalized relationship with the Lord God. They would be the messengers of hope for Israel to reconcile and return to their heavenly Father.

Understanding their concept of God was more critical for the disciples than everything else that followed the Lord's Prayer. If their concept of God was distorted, they would struggle with every challenge and responsibility Christ outlined in this spiritual blueprint for life and ministry.

If we call God our Father, we are to treat His name as holy. According to Jesus's explanation in Matthew 6:14-18, a proper response to His holiness, which is also as indispensable as forgiveness, is humility. Jesus established these qualities as two of the highest priorities in our relationship with the Father. One defines the Father's posture towards His people; the other defines His people's posture before Him. Together, these set the key expectations for a sustainable relationship with their heavenly Father.

This responsibility was so significant that Jesus stated that God's forgiveness was conditional and hinged on the willingness of His children to forgive others; if they refuse, then God will discipline His children for dishonoring their Father. The quality of their relationship with the Father would be reflected in how they treated others. The condition of their relationships with others would expose the character of their relationship with the Father.

But forgiveness is also inseparably connected to our love for God. To the degree that we truly value God's forgiveness, it will directly influence the scope of our love for Him. Consequently, our willingness to forgive others is also grounded and motivated by our love for people.

Humility is one of the most powerful characteristics for a child of God and arguably one of the more significant characteristics because He is holy. While forgiveness was how God drew near to the disciples, humility was an indispensable posture in how they were to move toward their heavenly Father. This was their foundation for life and ministry.

PRINCIPLES RELATED TO UNDERSTANDING GOD AS HEAVENLY FATHER:

1. The disciples called God their Father because He forgives. Since He is holy, forgiveness is the prerequisite to becoming family and one of the highest responsibilities of family relationships.

   - How well do you truly value God's holiness? How is that reflected in your life?
   - How does God's holiness shape the attitude of your own heart toward others?

2. One of the most important truths the disciples needed to keep at the forefront of their minds when they considered their heavenly Father's relationship to them was that He was a forgiving God.

   - What is the biggest challenge for you when it comes to forgiving others?
   - Why do you think Jesus taught on the responsibility to forgive so early in the prayer?

3. The disciples needed to approach God with humility.

   - What is your idea of humility?
   - How important is humility in a world filled with narcissism and entitlement?
   - How does humility find a place in your own life when the culture eagerly proclaims self-promotion?

4. Fasting was the most practical exercise for helping the disciples cultivate humility. Fasting was to be deeply personal and secluded from human eyes, to align their lives in fellowship with their heavenly Father.

   - Fasting, in our culture, is about weight loss and physical health? Have you ever practiced fasting in your relationship with your Heavenly Father?

- Why do you think Jesus emphasized humility above every other characteristic that could have been inserted in this narrative? Why?

PRAYER

Heavenly Father, thank you for the cleansing reality of Your forgiveness in my life. Your forgiveness was not only indispensable for me becoming Your child, but it is also vital to my ongoing relationship with You. Help me to fully embrace my identity as Your child, the freedom to know I am fully accepted by You, and your call to follow Your Son. Thank You for the freedom Your forgiveness brings to my life so that I might serve You fully.

Teach me to always show respect for your holy name. Help me live in a way that honors you. I never want to do anything that dishonors you, your name, or your kingdom's work on earth. I love you and desire to please you in everything. May my reputation with others be that my love for you is evident by the way I live and interact with others. In Jesus' holy name - Amen.

CHAPTER 3

YOUR KINGDOM, YOUR WILL.

How to Sync Your Life with Heaven's Mission

THY KINGDOM COME

> "Again, the devil took Him to a very high mountain and showed him all the kingdoms of the world and their glory; and he said to him, "All these I will give to you, if you fall down and worship me."

> Matthew 4:8-9

> "Thy Kingdom come; Thy will be done on earth as it is in heaven –"

> Matthew 6:10, NASB 1995

"Do not lay up for yourselves treasures on earth, where moth and rust destroy and where thieves break in and steal, but lay up for yourselves treasures in heaven, where neither moth nor rust destroys and where thieves do not break in and steal. For where your treasure is, there your heart will be also. The eye is the lamp of the body. So, if your eye is healthy, your whole body will be full of light, but if your eye is bad, your whole body will be full of darkness. If then the light in you is darkness, how great is the darkness! No one can serve two masters, for either he will hate the one and love the other, or he will be devoted to the one and despise the other. You cannot serve God and money."

Matthew 6:19-24

When I attended Briercrest Bible College in Caronport, Saskatchewan, one of the most popular books in the Christian marketplace was Garry Friesen's book, *Decision Making and the Will of God*. Discovering God's will was the hot topic of the day and one of the most talked-about issues outside of our college curriculum studies. For some, knowing God's will meant discovering His precise leading. Others appeared indifferent, feeling they had little to worry about because God would ensure His will would be done. Others felt a deep personal commitment to discerning His will through intimacy with Him in order to feel confident before acting.

This latter group was often accused of ignoring common sense and abandoning the clear teaching of the Word of God for a mystical experience. The pejorative cliché tagged to these practices was simply, "They are so heavenly-minded, they are no earthly good." They spent so much time trying to know God's will that they never became doers of His will. Knowing and doing His will was a real battle for me, even at this stage of my life.

I loved playing sports, but when I was departing for Briercrest, my mom had to talk me into taking my hockey equipment. I was convinced that I would never make the team because my talent would never keep up with real athletes. Admittedly, I was not really concerned about what God wanted me to do. After all, it was just playing hockey. But I struggled with my self-worth and did not want to be reminded I was not good enough when I did not make the team.

Briercrest was a bit of a "larger than life" experience. I decided to try out for the hockey team but made a huge blunder during the "tryouts." I made a comment to all these new-found friends that it would be fun to go try out for all the teams. What I meant, in my own mind, was coaches will let anyone try out for any of these teams but, eventually, they will cut most to keep the best. Since I was convinced I would not make any team, it would be fun, even surreal, to pretend to try out.

Unfortunately, most of the guys thought I was claiming to be an amazing athlete, and I could play on any team; they thought I was arrogant. It was not until my final year, sitting in the locker room getting ready for a hockey game, that one of my friends made an odd comment. He thought that I turned out ok in spite of his first impression that I was supremely arrogant. I was stunned.

But I learned I was presumptuously assuming God's will through my broken, dysfunctional thinking instead of trusting Him to reveal His will as I walked with Him. I created confusion and chaos for myself by making assumptions about what I thought would happen rather than trusting the Lord to show me what He wanted to happen. I was clearly thinking of myself rather than eternal priorities.

Jesus emphasized the need for a heavenly mindset, stating that being earthly-minded would render us ineffective. The challenge for Jesus was to keep His men focused on His kingdom program until the coming of the Father's kingdom, especially in light of His leaving. To keep them on mission, two critical priorities needed to become deep convictions in their lives. This was His purpose in Matthew 6:19-24.

EMBRACING A DIVINE PERSPECTIVE

The first priority was "storing up treasures in heaven," an expression related to keeping a divine perspective anchored to the future kingdom. The second was keeping a clear eye, which related to staying focused on always doing the Father's will. Faithfulness requires a state of mind firmly fixed on God's purpose since His kingdom program clashes with a world out of sync with its Creator.

An unwavering commitment to doing God's will is crucial to avoid falling into empty religious practices. Jesus taught the importance of maintaining focus on higher priorities to understand our roles and responsibilities in following Him. The first truth of the Lord's Prayer highlights God as life's defining priority. Life revolves around God's kingdom and will, emphasizing that everything begins and ends with Him. This demands embracing God's expectations as the standard for reality, choosing His values and priorities over personal beliefs. This mindset must affect how we spend money, engage in activities and hobbies, define our weekends, how we view people, interact with our neighbors, engage those we work with, and how we raise our families. This divine perspective must become more than wishful thinking, good intentions, or idealistic platitudes; it must shape our choices and behaviors. The tension is knowing the difference between a commitment to a way of life and the way we are to live.

The disciples had to grasp the tension between living in a world under Satan's dominion and God's authority. Satan offered Jesus universal rule over earthly kingdoms to avoid the cross. Despite the apparent opportunity, surrendering authority to Satan would have jeopardized God's righteousness. Satan's ambitions extended far beyond earthly kingdoms, aiming to become supreme over all, including God Himself. Satan's temptation of Jesus exposed his desire to undermine God, and Jesus's resilience emphasized the disciples' call to live in spiritual conflict.

In Matthew 6:19-24, Jesus explains key priorities to engage both His kingdom and His will. Verses 19-21 outline Christ's priorities related to God's kingdom. Verses 22-24 explain how His men were to succeed in knowing God's will. While these segments are a unified whole, these distinctions bring greater clarity to two critical components of the Lord's Prayer. They are, in fact, different sides of the same coin.

STORING UP TREASURES IN HEAVEN

The first priority of God's kingdom is a command to store up treasures in heaven. Jesus's play on words is powerful: "Do not treasure up treasures on earth, but treasure up for yourself treasures in heaven." What His disciples choose to do here on earth will make a difference in heaven. Our choices and actions on earth impact our ultimate experience in heaven. Our deeds not only contribute to God's kingdom here on earth, but also store up eternal benefits for ourselves. Like investing for retirement or providing an inheritance, an intentional commitment to eternal things has intense personal self-interest. Jesus stated it Himself: store up treasures *for yourself.*

Every disciple had the same opportunity to store up treasures in heaven. Jesus addressed the multitudes who lived in different parts of Israel. They belonged to different tribes and had various occupations. Regardless of social status or economic conditions, none of these factored into making an investment in eternal things.

Jesus's invitation reflects equality and inclusiveness with all who are children of God. Anyone who is part of God's family has the same free access to the Father. There is no hierarchy or special, privileged disciples. No one needs to be pre-qualified to store up treasures in heaven. However, this benefit is only for His children. No one outside of His family is entitled to these future and eternal rewards.

Jesus was a powerful teacher who communicated the reality of God's coming kingdom. He was careful to explain the critical values that would be the catalyst for godly commitment. Jesus shows that earthly resources are vital to God's kingdom work here on earth. He already highlighted spiritual qualities as preeminent in God's kingdom people, but earthly possessions were not unspiritual or unnecessary to His work here on earth (Matthew 5:3-16). Before understanding how to invest in treasures in heaven, Jesus taught His men that only those willing to embrace the right values will become fully invested in God's coming kingdom. Only these values provide the right orientation to produce active participants who will make a difference for God's eternal purpose.

BELIEFS AND VALUES

Obvious values are often hidden in plain sight. Our values must be anchored to our relationship with the Father. What we believe is true about our heavenly Father will shape our values, which will ultimately be reflected in our choices and behaviors. If, for example, we believe our Father forgives, the proof we truly value His forgiveness will be the freedom we experience from sin when we repent. If we truly believe He is holy, the proof will be seen in a growing attitude of humility.

What we believe directly influences our values, and our values reflect what we truly believe. Our actions expose our true values and, ultimately, validate our claim to what we believe. Actions speak louder than words and expose the true treasures of our hearts, whether they are treasures on earth or in heaven.

John was the forerunner of Jesus. He was preparing Israel for a radical transition of stepping away from religion to embracing God's personal ambassador who came to inaugurate a unique outworking of His kingdom on earth. The coming of God's Son was at the right moment, the right circumstance, and the most strategic divine appointment. Anyone who wanted to be welcomed into God's coming kingdom would need to embrace His Son. Only those who honored the Son would truly honor the Father. Those who rejected the Son would be rejected by the Father. Everyone who embraced Jesus would not only see His kingdom; they would be provided with what Peter described as an entrance into the eternal kingdom that will be abundantly supplied (2 Peter 1:11).

The only scenario for failure would be neglect. Unlike our limitations on earth, there is no limitation on how much treasure one can store in heaven. Each person has the freedom to put whatever time, energy, and resources into this investment as they choose, but it needs to be intentional and deliberate.

The most dangerous temptation to keep anyone from storing up treasures in heaven is the distraction of hoarding treasures on earth (Matthew 6:19). While there are other temptations and evils of which Christ's disciples must be aware, the distraction of earthly treasure is a unique obstacle to God's kingdom work.

Jesus specifically commanded His men not to store up treasures on earth because of the inevitable conflict of interest with His kingdom work. This obsession with treasures on earth was far more familiar than grasping the concept of eternal things. The nature of genuine faith is trusting the teaching of Jesus, not the practice of our culture.

Everyone understands the importance of providing for a family, leaving a legacy, and providing an inheritance. These ambitions are common among everyone. These necessities are reasonable and responsible expectations. The biblical expectation to look after our families cannot be ignored. But these acceptable pursuits need to be reconciled with Jesus's command not to store up treasures on earth. The obvious dilemma is calculating the difference between what we need compared to what we want.

To add more weight to His argument, Jesus would later explicitly command His disciples not to imitate the patterns of the Gentiles, who have made the accumulation of earthly resources the purpose of life (Matthew 6:32). They mastered the ability to store up treasures on earth, pursuing that which provides significance, security, and status in the world.

Jesus also called a handful of disciples to leave everything to follow Him (Matthew 19:27-30). He promised their sacrifice would not go unnoticed. They will sit on twelve thrones judging the twelve tribes of Israel (Matthew 19:28). Sacrificing everything to follow Jesus would be richly rewarded. One might assume these promises apply to a select group of special disciples, but Jesus also promised that anyone who left family, homes, and the security of these earthly treasures "shall receive many times as much and shall inherit eternal life" (Matthew 19:29, NASB1977). The challenge was not calculating how much they had to sacrifice but how much they could store up in heaven.

It begs the question of whether all cultural habits are biblically acceptable, at least to the Father, even when God's people find ways to justify them. Historically, many practices of God's people have become acceptable in Israel but completely unacceptable to God. The ongoing message of the prophets calling Israel to repentance is clear evidence that their practices did not find God's favor.

The fact that Jesus came preaching a gospel of repentance indicates that Israel was out of sync with the Lord they claimed to love and serve. As a starting point, Jesus set the standard later in verse 24 - we cannot serve two masters. If our pursuits, possessions, and priorities divide or distract us from serving Christ, then we are compelled to reassess our values.

The very essence of this coming kingdom was God the Father establishing His right to rule over His people and His creation. In the future, this heavenly kingdom would ultimately reveal God's glory. God would conquer the adversary, reclaim His people, and restore true righteousness. This was not a state of passive expectation, such as hope deferred. God inaugurated His kingdom program through His Son, who enlisted His disciples to carry out that kingdom work here on earth as the Father determined in heaven.

Jesus experienced this very tension in the wilderness. The devil offered Him all the kingdoms of the world and all their glory. We cannot underestimate the magnitude of such an offer. Ironically, Jesus would receive this glory anyway after his death and resurrection, but here, the devil tries to seduce Him with instant power, authority, and wealth apart from the way of the cross.[4] The devil's offering affirmed his dominion over the world. Yet it placed Jesus in a very real, spiritual dilemma that had massive implications.

Providing a shortcut to gain the very thing that only the cross could secure was monumental. These temptations were very real. Testing the Father, who was not able to sin, would be meaningless,

---

4 Blomberg, Craig. *Matthew*. Vol. 22, The New American Commentary, Broadman & Holman Publishers, 1992.

as Jesus reminded the devil during his second temptation (Matthew 4). Since Jesus, the God-Man, faced fundamental constraints of finite humanity like Adam and Eve, He was able not to sin. Yet, He had to make a choice that had apocalyptic and eternal implications, as universally far-reaching as the collateral damage that ensued from the choices of Adam and Eve.

Jesus taught His men to recognize their heavenly Father's kingdom was coming. His kingdom was the only treasure that would last. Everything else will perish. Their enthusiasm for this kingdom reached its peak when Jesus presented Himself alive after His sufferings. The disciples eagerly asked if Jesus was going to restore the kingdom to Israel (Acts 1:7). His death, resurrection, and ascension, however, delayed the full manifestation of that kingdom but launched an initiative for His kingdom program to make disciples of all nations (Matthew 28:18-20).

This kingdom included Israel, but Christ's death encompassed a greater kingdom program: a mission reaching the Gentiles. Paul explained it to the Colossians that the very nature of the gospel rescues men and women from the domain of darkness and transfers them to the kingdom of His beloved Son (Colossians 1:13). This was not just a future expectation but an active, intentional kingdom program Jesus entrusted to His men after He ascended to the Father.

"Treasures" refers to things of great value. Juxtaposing earthly treasures subject to decay, deterioration, and theft elevates heavenly treasures as an inheritance that are imperishable, undefiled, and unfading (2 Peter 1:11). Like God's wisdom, the least valuable thing in heaven will be exceedingly more valuable than the greatest treasures on earth. Yet the constant battle of the heart is being enamored with accumulating things on earth at the expense of the lasting value of the eternal.

The Scriptures do not define heavenly treasures in detail, but the nature of "heavenly things" is powerful. Even if the Bible was more specific, our minds would have serious limitations in grasping the full glory of eternal life, unrestrained and uninhibited by the afflictions in this life caused by sin and evil.

What is clear is that everything we see, smell, and touch here on earth is temporary. Everything we think is permanent will perish (2 Corinthians 4:18). We have become so attached to earthly things that it is hard to imagine something more glorious. His creation has been damaged so thoroughly that God will create a new heaven and earth, a place reserved only for those who are part of God's family (Revelation 21:1-3).

The only way to be part of his kingdom, to inherit eternal life is to be part of His family. No one who lives a good life goes to a better place. No human being is entitled to heaven. We all have eternal value because we are created in His image, but no one is good, and certainly not good enough before a holy God. Our good works can never save us. Sin has separated everyone from their Creator.

Every human being is infected by a spiritual disease that separates them from God's family. Heavenly treasures are experiencing life with God in paradise. The greatest treasures in His coming kingdom will be those men and women whom the disciples will help enter through the message of the gospel.

The demands of God's kingdom require a divine mindset focused on embracing these unseen treasures of heaven. The challenge is not just about a spiritual mindset but also about prioritizing resources. Resources are entrusted to us to further His kingdom work here on earth.

Jesus warns about every form of greed and reminds His listeners that even when one has an abundance of earthly things, life has far more significance than one's possessions (Luke 12:15). The parable of the rich landowner that captured the heart of Jesus warns that the one who stores up treasure for himself and is not rich toward God is a fool (Luke 12:20-21). One of the greatest pieces of evidence of our humility and faithfulness to our Father is a commitment to invest our resources in His kingdom and will.

What anyone truly values, they will pursue with their whole heart (Matthew 6:21). The heart is the seat of physical, spiritual, and mental life.[5] It is the center and the source of every aspect of the inner life. Separating what one treasures or values from the heart appears impossible, yet Jesus distinguishes the two.

Jesus is very particular in His wording. In Matthew 6:21, Jesus did not say, "Where your heart is, there your treasure will be." Western culture separates logic and emotion. Generally speaking, the mind is for logic and rational thought, and the heart is for emotion. Jesus appears to do a similar thing here.

The faithfulness of God's children is not about following our hearts, which is the mantra of many Christians. The heart can be attracted to a multitude of things, and many of those things are not considered wrong in and of themselves. Misplaced devotion and the pursuit of things can become the toxic idols of our passion. If earthly treasures capture one's heart, every disciple becomes a victim of earthly distractions.

These idols can mislead even the sincerest believer. Paul reminded Timothy that the love of money is a root of all kinds of evils. It is through this craving that some have wandered away from the faith and pierced themselves with many pangs (1 Timothy 6:10). This was the deepest concern of Jesus for His men living

---

5 Arndt, William, et al. *A Greek-English Lexicon of the New Testament and Other Early Christian Literature.* 3rd ed., University of Chicago Press, 2000, p. 508.

in a broken world: to be in the world and to be conformed to its distractions.

Kingdom values need to shape the desires of our hearts, not the other way around. Even the Psalmist understood these distinctions: "Delight yourself in the Lord, and he will give you the desires of your heart" (Psalm 37:4). The responsibility is to choose to value the Lord, therefore being rewarded by receiving the desires of our hearts.

Everyone will always make time and effort for things they truly value; people will always put their whole hearts into what they ultimately treasure. To pursue things that attract the heart first can lead to a double-minded life. This is the exact concern of Matthew 6:24 about divided loyalties. But when one chooses to delight in the things of the Lord, God promises to give them the desires of their heart.

All that being said, Jesus challenged His disciples that kingdom values take precedence over the earthly attractions, and deeply held values truly shape the heart. In short, we have often heard the saying, "Someone can be so heavenly-minded that they are no earthly good." *Jesus has made it very clear that a disciple who is not heavenly-minded will be of no earthly good!*

Examining one's commitments will inevitably reveal one's values. When one supports the other, actions speak louder than words. Anyone can claim something is important to them, but only their actions validate that claim. The issue is not that we do not have enough time but that our values shape how we use our time. When some things take up our time, either out of necessity or choice, it does not mean those things we do not finish are unimportant; we simply have other things we value more.

While heavenly values are indispensable to kingdom life, another element of Jesus's commentary is necessary to turn values into actual commitment. Without this component, values crumble under the inertia of wishful thinking. The only way to stay true to one's values was to remain fixed on God's will.

"Thy will be done on earth, as it is in heaven."

Matthew 6:10, KJV

"The lamp of the body is the eye; if therefore your eye is clear, your whole body will be full of light. But if your eye is bad, your whole body will be full of darkness. If therefore the light that is in you is darkness, how great is the darkness! No one can serve two masters; for either he will hate the one and love the other, or he will hold to one and despise the other. You cannot serve God and mammon."

Matthew 6:22-24, NKJV

God's kingdom is inseparable from God's will, but God's will is more than just His kingdom. Jesus taught His men to pray for the Father's coming kingdom *and* to pray for God's will to be done on earth as God purposed it in heaven. Until the Father's kingdom comes fully, His kingdom work needs to be done until it is fully revealed. This is the focus of His will being done on earth. His will clearly needs to be consistent and connected to His coming kingdom, making the gospel of the kingdom one of the clear priorities of doing His will.

In verses 22-24, Jesus offers an ingenious perspective that helps His disciples realize that discerning God's will is more important than knowing all of God's will. Two ingredients are essential to doing God's will: first, God needs to communicate His expectations for how His children ought to live, and second, we need to maintain focus on those expectations in order to remain committed to them.

We all have one master, who is our Father in heaven, and we are to serve Him and do His will. According to Jesus, the key to understanding this is having a clear focus on the things that our Father values above all else.

THE KEY TO SUCCESSFUL KINGDOM LIFE

One of the biggest challenges my wife Barb and I had before I asked her to marry me was that my desire for ministry conflicted with her experiences as a missionary kid. She grew up on the mission field, which provided many opportunities to grow her faith but also had its challenges. She grew up swearing she would never marry anyone in ministry. However, I believed God had called me to the ministry, so we had an impasse.

Love does strange things to us. Barb assured me that she would abandon her oath to never marry anyone in ministry because she loved me. I did not buy that she could so easily set aside her conviction to not get caught in that life again, so we had to talk. I was unrelenting in my conviction that God called me to ministry. I drew a line in the sand, saying that if she could not be supportive of being in full-time ministry, then we should not get married.

We have now been married for almost forty years, so we obviously worked out the dilemma. Yet our first year married, like most couples, was one of our most difficult and challenging years together. We walked straight into a small village church in central Alberta immediately after returning from our honeymoon. We not only had to adjust to marriage, but we also immediately launched into full-time ministry in a rural context with no family around. The multitude of changes and adapting to a strange world with which we were not familiar created tremendous strain and stress in our relationship.

Regardless of these challenges, the one thing that helped us was the resolve to keep our eyes firmly fixed on what God had called us to do. This was far from being a cliché. If we were not firmly convinced of His purpose and had previously resolved that this was not negotiable, it would have been easy to allow these distractions and tensions to push me into another profession.

UNDERSTANDING GOD'S WILL

Jesus explained to His men that the eye is the lamp of the body (Matthew 6:22). The formula is simple: if their eye was healthy, their life would be full of light. A healthy eye or person is someone motivated by singleness of purpose so as to be open and aboveboard, without guile, sincere, and straightforward. A life full of light is lived by someone with the highest integrity and character.

A clear eye did not have anything to do with physical health. Jesus was not warning about a physical eye disease like macular degeneration, cataracts, or detached retinas that would impede the ability to see clearly. However, the metaphor served well to communicate a critical truth to give insight into the spiritual health of their heart.

Having a clear eye was about perspective and focus. The admonition is about seeing God clearly and understanding the nature of being in relationship with Him. Our whole identity is to be shaped by this relationship, changing the way we view ourselves and others. It is about spiritual health to keep both our relationship with our Father vibrant *and* being faithfully obedient to His Word. A clear eye embraces a certain worldview defined by God Himself.

A clear eye views the world through the eyes of our heavenly Father, not our own. Only His perspective allows us to see reality the way God sees it. A clear eye has a genuine Biblical perspective not hampered by human finiteness and brokenness. Clarity is only possible when we see our own lives, and all lives, from the viewpoint of the only One who has ultimate objectivity. It is impossible to have a clear eye apart from a relationship with the Lord. It is God's responsibility to reveal His will to His people. He promises to guide His children and provide what we need to serve and worship Him well. The primary source for an obedient life is God's revealed Word.

Through the Law, Israel had everything they needed. They did not have to guess what God expected. He gave clear instructions about their relationship with Him, with each other, and how they were to be distinct from the nations around them. They simply needed to keep their eyes fixed on His truth and their hearts rooted in His loyal love.

LIVING WITH CLEAR EYES

A person with clear eyes is someone who clings to their relationship with their heavenly Father. The first issue that demands clarity and focus is to see the Lord God not just as a sovereign, omnipotent being but to see Him as our heavenly Father. While previously noted, it was vital for Israel to see a God who was personal, who cared for them and did everything for their good. God's self-revelation defined His essential nature of their heavenly Father:

> "The LORD, the LORD God, compassionate and gracious, slow to anger, and abounding in lovingkindness and truth, who keeps lovingkindness for thousands, who forgives iniquity, transgression, and sin; yet He will by no means leave the guilty unpunished, visiting the iniquity of fathers on their children and on the grandchildren to the third and fourth generation."
>
> Exodus 34:6-7, NASB1995

Their identity as children of God defined their existence in the world. The more clarity they had about God's character and commitment to them, the more confident they were in their ability to live in the world. If they lost sight of who God was, they would lose sight of their significance as His children living in the world.

A clear eye will live for God's kingdom and His kingdom work on earth. God's kingdom work on earth is the new paradigm for how God's children are to live. This is the new lens that shapes others' perspectives. People are not valued by social distinctions, ethnic prejudices, or any other distinction. Jesus shows the eternal value of all humanity, not just one tribe.

God's eternal purpose takes precedence over earthly ambitions. His kingdom work motivated His disciples when they got up in the morning. It was their impetus for spending time with people and the catalyst for serving others. Their occupations, hobbies, callings, and passions revolved around investing in and expanding God's kingdom in the world. In any other terms, they had an eternal perspective on a temporal world.

All other earthly success diminishes in light of the need for the gospel of the kingdom. God's children are ambassadors in the world and are entrusted with a ministry of reconciling the world back to the Father. This does not mean that God's children are to reject the world, but they were not to become like the world. We do not isolate ourselves from the world but live godly lives within the world.

LIVING WITH A BAD EYE

Conversely, if our eyes are bad, we live in darkness. The term "bad" carries the weight of something being evil. Anything that is not in harmony with the light is evil. Darkness is associated with spiritual blindness and being unresponsive to the true light of Christ. But a bad eye is not necessarily evil as most would conceive it. A bad eye may simply be an attempt to rely on one's own perspective rather than seeing life from our heavenly Father's viewpoint.

The god of this world has blinded the eyes of the world, so many do not see this God we call Father. Everyone outside His family lives in darkness and ignorance of the true nature of their Creator. Those who genuinely seek to honor God will defer their success in the world for reflecting their Father's character to the world.

The first casualty of a bad eye and this internal darkness is a person's relationship with their heavenly Father. A bad eye simply means they have diverted their focus from their Father to other things that captured their attention. Their love for the Father is exchanged for a love for things or other temporal attractions, regardless if it is related more to power, wealth, significance, or anything that stole their heart from their Father. His forgiveness stops translating into forgiving others, and consequently, they lose sight of the value of people. Humility surrenders to self-confidence and independence from the Father. They lose sight of doing everything with a view to honoring their Father.

Instead of "storing up treasures in heaven," they will quickly fall to the temptation of storing up treasures only for themselves. The lure for independence and personal significance began to cloud their vision of investing in their Father's priorities. This darkness may not always be exposed by moral compromise or self-destructive behavior. It means that they serve a different master, and God's kingdom work fades into the background of the frenetic pace of self-sufficiency.

This does not mean neglecting normal responsibilities of life. The Bible tells us that we need to be responsible for providing for our family (1 Timothy 5:8). We need to do excellent work in our occupations (Colossians 3:23). The danger in life is becoming so preoccupied with our own priorities that God's kingdom takes a back seat to doing our own thing. Paul made this case when he talked about marriage:

> "I want you to be free from anxieties. The unmarried man is anxious about the things of the Lord, how to please the Lord. But the married man is anxious about worldly things, how to please his wife, and his interests are divided. And the unmarried or betrothed woman is anxious about the things of the Lord, how to be holy in body and spirit. But the married woman is anxious about worldly things, how to please her husband."
>
> 1 Corinthians 7:32-34

Even good things can divert one's focus, and worldly things can divide our interests. To the extent which this contributes to having a bad eye might be arguable, but the principle is the same. Satan tempted Jesus to turn stones into bread, but the end does not justify the means. The preoccupation with building our own kingdom overwhelms the investment in the eternal purpose of the Father. We might continue to give lip service to these spiritual priorities, but the danger is these things amount to nothing more than moral support rather than a way of life. This is the concern and warning of Matthew 6:24:

> "No one can serve two masters; for either he will hate the one and love the other, or he will hold to one and despise the other. You cannot serve God and money."

Essentially, a bad eye is one that has divided allegiance between the eternal priorities of God's call and the distraction of the things of this world.

WHEN THE TWO BECOME ONE

When I was twelve years old, my parents took me to the public course near our home for golf lessons. Five group lessons later, the course gave us a free round of golf. That was the first time I played on a real golf course, and I shot 12 over par, 82 on 18 holes. Something about the personal challenge combined with learning a skill and being outdoors just captured my imagination. I instantly fell in love with the game.

That summer, Mom and Dad bought me a season pass that cost only $25.00, and I played all summer long. I lived and breathed golf. I played 54 holes of golf every day, three full rounds of golf for four solid months. No one made me do this; I was intensely self-motivated. If I was not required to be anywhere else, I would get up early, have Mom drive me to the course, and I would come home at about nine o'clock that night. In the simplest terms, I wrapped my whole life around the game of golf.

I read magazines about golf, studied putting strategy, practiced my swing all the time, and even bought a hitting net for the backyard. I was, for all intents and purposes, obsessed with the game. I even played with the idea of going to school in the United States to be able to find a place I could play all year round because I wanted to become a professional. I still love to golf, but I hardly get any time to play. In fact, at this stage of life, the only time I do play is when we are on vacation. I value playing, but my eye is focused on many other things.

To help understand the nature of the relationship between values (treasures) and perspectives (clear eye), these can be compared to personal hobbies.

Hobbies are activities people passionately love to do. In some mysterious way, the very nature of these activities produces an energy of deep attraction in the invisible nature of a person's inner being. Something triggers intensely felt values and clear focus for some activity or cause. Values and clear perspective synchronize to produce an unstoppable passion.

Anyone with an enthusiastic hobby will put almost limitless amounts of time, energy, and resources to experience the thrill that activity stirs within his or her heart. If we could transfer our passion and focus from our hobbies to our Father's kingdom work, it could radically transform the level of our commitment and multiply our impact.

Not only is God's kingdom worthy of such devotion, but the power of His personal presence ought to be the most powerful, energizing force compelling His people to serve Him in the world.

This was what Jesus explained to His disciples about storing up treasures in heaven and keeping their eyes firmly fixed on God's will. Together, in some mysterious manner, these two key elements will produce an unquenchable passion that is as all-consuming as an obsession. The disciple who has these eternal values firmly implanted in their heart and keeps their eye fixed on God's purpose is as passionate about the relationship with their heavenly Father and His kingdom work as any person consumed with his or her favorite hobby.

Why doesn't our commitment to Christ match the energy we put into our favorite hobbies? The time we put into social media, or the focus we give to endless hours of video games or our favorite sports activity, often outperforms the energy we put into our relationship with our heavenly Father. *When our values and focus are in alignment, commitment is thrilling. But when they are out of alignment, everything is a challenge.* This would explain why some things that ought to have high value to us are such a struggle and things that are fleeting seem to get our full attention.

The simplest answer is that while we value heavenly things, our eyes are full of distractions. Our passion has been disconnected from our values and redirected to other things. We might have our sight fixed on His will, but we have been distracted by earthly treasures.

Jesus's final explanation was exactly to this point. No one can serve two masters. Jesus was not challenging His disciples about hobbies; He was charging them about what master they would ultimately serve. His final statement, "You cannot serve God and money," defined the two masters between which His disciples ultimately had to choose. Money or mammon is the power of earthly treasures and the source of virtually all earthly treasures in one form or another. The other choice is God. These are not false alternatives but the reality of storing up treasures in heaven or pursuing earthly things.

When our values and our focus are not on the same target, we create a divided allegiance. Jesus describes this as loving one master and hating the other. Mammon is not only connected to the basic idea of treasures on earth, but it carries with it the idea of a false worship. The reminder within Matthew 6:24 is the impossibility of serving two masters. Even our earthly treasures or wealth can challenge God's right to rule over our lives. We cannot serve God and mammon.

Our actions speak louder than words. We need to evaluate our behaviors and practices, not our claims. We have convinced ourselves our status quo is acceptable to God. If we are genuinely honest with ourselves, we have lost sight of the true value of His kingdom work and the unmatched privilege we have to participate in God's divine purpose. We may value eternal things, but our eyes are fixed on temporal things. We have divided our allegiance by trying to serve two masters. To make matters worse, we have blamed others for our own internal struggle by exempting ourselves from any responsibility.

Maybe our prayer needs to be one of confession about our selfishness. We have spent far more investing in treasures on earth than in His coming kingdom. Our claim to love Jesus has been diminished by our passion for things on earth. Through confession and forgiveness, we can evaluate our values and regain our perspective that we might truly invest in storing up treasures in heaven.

PRINCIPLES ABOUT HIS COMING KINGDOM:

1. God's kingdom involves embracing two critical elements: values and focus. When these two elements come together, they will inevitably produce commitment. One cannot survive without the other.

   - How does the relationship between values and focus help you understand why commitment to some things is such a struggle for you?
   - How do you normally operate when it comes to making choices: do you follow your heart, or do you make decisions based on eternal values?

2. What a person truly values is where their heart will be. Conversely, when we chase only those things that attract our heart, we may grab what we want, but it may not be what God desires. God has called us to value eternal things and allow our hearts to follow.

   - What areas of your relationship with your heavenly Father do you struggle with the most?
   - Good intentions always get crushed under the weight of our true values. What good intentions have never been fulfilled in your life? Why?

3. We can never serve two masters. We will love one and hate the other. If we value the treasures of this world more than the eternal things of God's kingdom, it will be impossible to live a God-honoring life.

   - What things in your life divide your commitment to Christ?
   - Which commitments get more of your energy - storing up treasure in heaven or on earth?

- What would need to change in you to faithfully pursue "treasures in heaven"?

4. A God-honoring life values eternal things and keeps one's focus on what ultimately matters. A true disciple keeps his or her eye on their relationship with God and his or her responsibility to His kingdom.

  - How challenging is it for you to be motivated by eternal things you cannot see?
  - How comfortable are you with changing your behaviors and habits to make eternal things? Why or why not?

5. What can you learn from your favorite hobby that would be a good example of what kind of commitment Jesus asks you to make to His kingdom and do His will?

  - Why is it so easy for you to put time into your favorite hobby?
  - We often use external things to motivate us to change. What does Jesus make clear about true change to embrace His will?
  - Since actions speak louder than words, how does your commitment to God's kingdom compare to your commitment to your favorite hobby?

PRAYER

Lord, help me value Your kingdom here on earth as You would desire in heaven. May Your Spirit keep on reminding me of the things that will ultimately last. Teach me to store up treasure in heaven by investing my life in Your kingdom work here on earth. Help me grasp that values alone do not translate into commitment, and I need to fix my eyes on those things You say are of the greatest importance. My actions and investments reveal what I truly value and fix my attention. Amen.

CHAPTER 4

DAILY BREAD, DAILY GRIND

Trusting God to Show Up in Your Everyday

"Give us this day, our daily bread."

Matthew 6:11

"For this reason, I say to you, do not be anxious for your life, as to what you shall eat, or what you shall drink; nor for your body, as to what you shall put on. Is not life more than food, and the body than clothing? Look at the birds of the air, that they do not sow, neither do they reap, nor gather into barns, and yet your heavenly Father feeds them. Are you not worth much more than they? And which of you, by being anxious, can add a single cubit to his life's span? And why are you anxious about clothing? Observe how the lilies of the field grow; they do not toil, nor do they spin, yet I say to you that even Solomon in all his glory did not clothe himself like one of these. But if God so arrays the grass of the field, which is alive today and tomorrow is thrown into the furnace, will He not much more do so for you, O men of little faith?"

Matthew 6:25-30, NASB1977

O ne of the fortunate provisions for our family growing up was that my dad worked in the oil industry. He was the Manager of Tax for one of the largest oil companies in Canada. We lived simple lives on a side street in the suburbs of the Westgate community. We lived in a 1,200-square-foot, three-bedroom ranch-style house with a nice backyard on a quiet, neighbor-friendly street. We never lacked anything. Dad did not give much away, but he made sure that we could participate in school activities, community sports, and personal hobbies.

The idea of not having what we needed never crossed our minds as kids. Our parents had their challenges, but they cared about one another, and they cared about us. The idea of worrying about having enough food or not having a place called home never was a point of concern.

While the United States has recorded that 87% of households are secure regarding food, almost 21 percent of households in America deal with some level of food insecurity. In 2021, the world statistics indicated that almost 2.3 billion are moderately or severely food insecure. The contributing factors are extensive, including rising inflation, economic turmoil, and regional instability, to name a few, but all influence these extreme circumstances. While some people can hardly imagine such uncertainties, others live with them daily.[6]

---

6 United States Department of Agriculture, Economic Research Service. "Food Security and Nutrition Assistance." *Ag and Food Statistics: Charting the Essentials*, www.ers.usda.gov/data-products/ag-and-food-statistics-charting-the-essentials/food-security-and-nutrition-assistance/ Accessed 7 Dec. 2024.

The simple truth is that the fact that the Lord trained His men to ask their heavenly Father to provide daily bread is often undermined by its ambiguity. Regardless of the cultural differences from our own, the first-century culture had poor and rich households, cost of living, and inflation; they still had to deal with inequities in their communities. But in our current affluence in American culture, some are convinced God does not keep this particular promise while others deem this simple request as completely irrelevant to their own circumstances.

This does not mean there are not many who struggle with food insecurity for numerous reasons in our culture and around the world. But the uber-abundance of many cultures, like our own, may render the very thought of depending on God for daily needs essentially meaningless. We readily have at our fingertips an abundance of basic needs like food, drink, and clothing; these resources seem endless. But when these basic needs are not being met, even Christians have questioned God's integrity regardless of situation or circumstance.

The more subtle deception for even sincere disciples has been the ongoing dedication of life to the mass accumulation of the most basic needs of life. The abundance of food, massive and ostentatious shelters, and the rapid pursuit of excess may be one of the most detrimental temptations that most Christians have succumbed to quite unintentionally.

Men and women process stress differently. That might not be much of a revelation, but men often claim that they do not worry. Even in the most stressful situations, many will rarely admit that they are anxious. Guys tend to have a very stoic approach to life and are adamant they do not worry when everyone else is an emotional train wreck. The way one figures out if men are anxious about anything is not how they feel but how much they think about something. If a man isn't sleeping at night, it is often because he has been grinding on a problem, figuring out a solution, or fixing a dilemma, and that is a male version of anxiety.

Women, on the other hand, are wired differently and often are more honest about their anxiety. They will talk out their anxiety and even feel a sense of panic if they think something might happen to someone they love. Ladies often have a different way of processing than men, and it is usually more transparent.

Jesus's first temptation in the wilderness was to turn stones into bread. He had fasted 40 days and nights. He was in starvation mode. His basic need for food is a fundamental need for all human beings. Everyone can go for short periods without food and even less time without water. These are not luxuries; these are basic human necessities. Without these, we will simply die.

We have a cultural expression for individuals who get cranky when they get hungry: "hangry." After 40 days and nights, most of us would have been delirious! In some ways, the offer from the devil to make bread hardly seems to qualify as a temptation. Could there be anything wrong with Jesus performing a miracle to provide for His own needs, especially when it would not hurt anyone, violate a law, or, under the circumstances, be considered self-centered?

However, the devil changed everything with one simple statement: "If you are the Son of God, turn these stones into bread." He called Jesus's relationship to the Father into question and challenged Jesus to prove the viability of the claim to be the Son of God. He challenged the significance of His relationship with the Father and His identity.

By using His need for food as leverage, He provoked Jesus to take matters into His own hands and put His personal interests before the Father's will. The innuendo questioned the Father's care and provision by allowing Jesus to go through such hardship. The nature of this temptation indirectly accused God of betrayal. It was the Spirit of God who led Jesus into the wilderness for the very purpose of being tempted. The insinuation was that the Father did not care for the Son and was negligent in providing for Him.

The devil leveraged even the most fundamental human need to tempt Jesus into evil. The devil played by his own rules, and he had no problem exploiting any human finiteness to distract Christ from the Father's purpose. Nowhere can this be seen more dramatically in the Scriptures than his attack on Job.

God permitted the devil to touch all the essential needs in Job's life (Job 1:12). The devil afflicted his health, his family, and his wealth. These hardships created massive strain on his friendships and even his relationship with his spouse. His wife even told Job to curse God and die! God acknowledged that Satan had incited him against Job to ruin him without cause (Job 2:3). Fewer things have the potential to destroy the credibility of relationships with others and with God than when affliction touches our basic human needs.

Jesus' temptation provoked Him to include this very simple request when He taught His men to pray. He knew the devil would leverage these essential needs to blindside the disciples as they sought to follow Christ and serve Him. The devil would do anything to destroy God's kingdom and His purpose. But how the devil weaponizes these basic needs can only be understood when Jesus explained the implications of this request:

"Do not be anxious then, saying 'What shall we eat? Or what shall we drink? Or with what shall we clothe ourselves? For these things the Gentiles eagerly seek; for your heavenly Father knows that you have need of all these things... But seek first

His kingdom and His righteousness; and all these things shall be added to you. Therefore, do not be anxious for tomorrow; for tomorrow will care for itself. Each day has enough trouble of its own."

Matthew 6:25-34, NASB1977

The request in the Lord's Prayer asking the Father for daily bread implies relying on Him for the essentials of life: food, drink, and clothing (Matthew 6:25). Depending on your context, this aspect of the prayer makes sense if you live with some degree of food insecurity. However, it may seem irrelevant because God does not seem interested in answering such a request, or you would not be living with food insecurity.

On the other hand, if you have never lacked anything, the prayer may seem to be essentially irrelevant. Asking God to provide for something when we have no lack seems to be a mere religious ritual with little to no substance in the real world. Oddly enough, those very responses to this simple prayer seem to be the best evidence for the absolute necessity for it!

Even a casual survey of the Scriptures ought to impress upon us that there are fewer things in life that leave humanity more vulnerable than when Satan exploits our basic needs to tempt us to live selfishly. Adam and Eve cast all humanity under a curse over a piece of fruit. When Israel took possession of the Promised Land, they eventually abandoned God because they lacked nothing.

Satan's most strategic attack on Jesus in the wilderness was leveraging His desperate need for food to put Himself before the Father's purpose. Satan loves manipulating human limitations to drag them away from relying on their heavenly Father.

The most basic point of this simple request is to acknowledge, at the very least, that God Himself is the One who has provided for the fundamental needs of all human beings. Regardless of the process or the work of humanity, God Himself created a world in which mankind is to care for the world, and the world was created to provide for all humanity.

God cared for Jesus's disciples as a Father would care for His own children. He promised to care for them and provide for their needs. They were to depend on their Father as the ultimate provider for all they needed. But living in the real world, there are innumerable challenges where basic needs go unmet because of any number of extenuating circumstances. A lack of provision can tempt us to be frustrated with God, while an overabundance of provisions can tempt us to forget about Him.

THE DANGER OF ANXIETY

Jesus desired to explain the significance of the spiritual principle related to this simple portion of the prayer so that it would not be easily misunderstood or dismissed. If His people were to understand both the power of this request and the inherent danger Jesus addressed, it would require His insight and wisdom. Jesus spoke to one of the most subtle threats to the disciples as they sought to know the Father's will and participate in His kingdom work.

Anxiety and worry become deadly leverage points when exposed to the devil. Satan manipulates our need to create fear of future insecurity. He mastered the ability to get people to worry about a hundred worst-case scenarios that never happen just to bury our hearts in a quagmire of anxiety. All this is done to destroy faith in what God has promised to do for His children.

Jesus commanded His disciples to not be anxious about their basic needs of life. The concept of anxiety is to have an anxious concern based on apprehension about possible danger or misfortune. One of the clearest examples of anxiety is in Matthew 10:19, when Jesus told His men He was sending them as sheep amongst wolves. He warned that they would be persecuted and dragged before human courts, governors, and kings for His sake. But He charged them not to be anxious about what they would say to their persecutors because the Lord would give them the words to speak.

The very nature of anxiety may seem completely legitimate in the face of such circumstances. They lived in an uncertain world, and since they were representing Jesus in a hostile world, being in harm's way was a real danger. One might argue that it is not realistic not to be anxious about these things in the tumultuous world in which they lived!

FAITH AND FOOD

Jesus illustrated the Father's care for His children by using two illustrations from nature. The first example was related to God's provision for food, illustrated by His care for birds. They have no capacity to do things humans would intuitively engage in. They have no ability to sow, they do not have the aptitude to reap crops, nor the ingenuity to store up food, and yet the Father provides food for them. These creatures have no capacity to provide for themselves, but regardless, the Father cares enough about them. He provides for their basic need for food.

His second illustration is to convince them not to be anxious about clothing. This time, He used the lilies of the field. These were most likely wildflowers that grew anywhere and everywhere in this area of the world. Jesus compares their beauty, reflecting the artistic hand of the Father, with Solomon in all His glory. These flowers are far more spectacular in Jesus's eyes than Solomon's most remarkable achievements.

Jesus emphasized three critical truths to His disciples. First, life is far more than food or clothing. This statement implies that many try to build the significance of life around such things as food or clothing. Thus, success is defined by the quality and quantity of such goods. Any reflection on the prestige of the nations reveals that much of the mass production of goods and services centers on basic human needs.

Secondly, their lives were far more valuable to the Father than those of creatures like the birds of the air. The specific reference to God as their heavenly Father is a strong reminder that they belonged to His family. He cares for His children with far more zeal than other creatures. God's people have a special place in the heart of God, and He is committed to always being present in order to provide for His children.

Thirdly, Jesus pointed out that even though the flowers of the field have a magnificence far greater than any wonder of the world accomplished by mankind, their existence is fleeting. They are alive one day and the next thrown away, and yet the Father cares about the flowers of the field and the birds of the air. But the Father's care for people is exponentially superior to His concern for these created things. The anxiety that caused a struggle to believe God would provide for them was a clear demonstration of a lack of faith (Matthew 6:30). We are also reminded that our lives, like the flowers of the field, are fleeting. James described even the rich man as one who, like the grass of the field, will also pass away (James 1:9-10).

The only time the concept of faith surfaces in the Sermon on the Mount is in this text. The only time "faith" surfaces in the Lord's Prayer, and even in Jesus's explanation through chapters six and seven, is here. *Of all the critical issues Jesus deals with in the Lord's Prayer, all of which we might assume must demand a radical faith, this is the only place Jesus explicitly brings up the necessity of faith.* Many might not think faith is necessary, much less indispensable, to depend on the Lord for daily needs.

These provisions are so automated in our lives that it would take a miracle for most to consistently ask God to provide these daily needs. This is precisely why Jesus talked about values and focus before he dealt with food and clothing. Nothing can dull a disciple's heart toward their heavenly Father more quickly than the scarcity of basic needs or the over-abundance of the same.

THE ADVERSITY OF ANXIETY

Jesus pointed out that anxiety over these kinds of things changes nothing in life, or more specifically, anxiety cannot add a single hour to our lives. The better part of practical wisdom demonstrates that anxiety robs people of life and becomes exhausting, fearing what often never comes to fruition. Nothing has more power to destroy the vitality of life than anxiety.

Anxiety does more than suck away the vitality and joy of life; it also undermines our relationship with our heavenly Father. Dependence on the Father to provide for His children is weakened by constant worry about the very things the Father promises to supply. Jesus took considerable time to address the issue of anxiety as related to daily needs. Clearly, He understands the vital significance of how Satan leveraged these things to deceive Christ's followers. He is strategically committed to damage our confidence in God's care.

While anxiety over food insecurity, as we would express it, appears to be the basic focus of the text, there is value in understanding that there are other dimensions of anxiety with which we struggle in today's world.

When we think about anxiety related to food, our thoughts generally focus on food insecurity since that tends to be the most prevalent public concern. But there are other dynamics of anxiety that circle around basic needs, particularly food, that generate other forms of worry. These anxieties are connected to deeper issues within the invisible brokenness of a person's heart, and it is mirrored by the pursuits of the Gentiles.

Jesus's final caveat is against the practices of the Gentiles, who made the eager pursuit of these basic needs their ambition. In the context of His explanation, the implication is the deep-seated, core motivation of the Gentiles for such a radical accumulation of earthly goods is the anxiety of not having them or not having enough of them.

While the purpose might seem self-evident, there is value in recognizing these things which represent a status symbol of significance and success. The world's obsession with these things immediately brings to mind Jesus's warning back in Matthew 6:25 that life cannot be defined by how many of these basic needs one possesses; life is more than these things. The challenge, of course, was if the disciples would believe it.

Yet, the Gentiles were passionately committed to accumulating these things in abundance. Certainly, the power to accumulate and store an abundance of resources demonstrated a certain status of success in almost any culture: it indicated resourcefulness, ingenuity, self-sufficiency, power, and success. Christ warned His men they were not to be like them.

THE AFFLICTION OF ANXIETY

But this eager pursuit of self-worth and significance has also produced, at least in our culture, additional complications related to the problem of anxiety. Anxiety affects men and women differently. According to the National Institute of Mental Health (NIMH), in the United States, the prevalence of anxiety disorders is about twice as high in women compared to men.[7] The reality of our culture is

---

7 McLean, Carmen P et al. "Gender differences in anxiety disorders: prevalence, course of illness, comorbidity and burden of illness." *Journal of psychiatric research* vol. 45,8 (2011):

that we are plagued by numerous afflictions cultivated by anxiety, resulting in a wide spectrum of disorders including panic disorder, social anxiety disorder, and a variety of phobia-related disorders.

One of the most typical anxieties is anorexia nervosa or bulimia nervosa. These both are related to the quantity of food one consumes. Anorexia is related to the lack of food and thus places oneself in the desperate condition of starvation. The physical consequences are only a shadow of the internal struggle. The invisible afflictions of the mind are the battleground where anxiety triumphs over common sense, logic, and theology.

Bulimia is about overeating or gorging oneself and then purging behaviors that expel food. The most commonly agreed-upon symptoms include psychological factors, including low self-esteem, body dissatisfaction, perfectionism, and mood disorders like depression or anxiety. Biological factors like genetics also appear to contribute to a person's vulnerability to this disorder and create a higher risk for certain individuals. Sociological factors related to cultural ideals of beauty, body image, and acceptance also contribute to the deception of taking extreme measures to validate self-worth, significance, and security by defining life on their own. All these factors stem from anxiety that is manifested in the basic needs of life but point to the deeper issues of the heart.

Clearly, defining the meaning of life by temporal elements or successes of this world will always be deficient. Jesus's prayer ought to anchor His disciples to the true source of identity, significance, and security. Any other source outside of our Creator to fulfill these fundamental needs of our existence will always be found wanting. Jesus' prayer anchored his disciples to the true source of identity, significance, and security. The only source for a clear understand-

1027-35. doi:10.1016/j.jpsychires.2011.03.006

ing of our value and worth is inseparably anchored to our relationship with our heavenly Father and being a child of God.

Instead of being anxious about having enough or trying to define our self-worth and significance by these temporary, first-world issues, Jesus sets a higher priority. The disciples were to seek first the Father's kingdom and His righteousness, and then God would provide what they needed, not what they desired or wanted.

FINDING FREEDOM FROM ANXIETY

Jesus taught His men to pray for the Father's kingdom to come and His will to be done on earth. Our lives are not to be consumed with worrying about basic needs. We need to have confidence that our heavenly Father would care for us. If His kingdom is coming, then we are to keep on seeking His kingdom and His righteousness.

The same root word that Jesus uses to describe the Gentiles, "eagerly seeking" after an abundance of these basic needs, is the same term Jesus uses to command His disciples "to keep on seeking" after Father's kingdom and righteousness. Jesus uses the passion and commitment of the Gentiles who eagerly sought to stockpile basic provision as a model for how His disciples ought to be seeking after the Father's purpose. Faithful disciples will put the same energy and effort into God's kingdom and righteousness as the Gentiles do into their life pursuits.

But there is even a deeper problem for God's people associated with food, drink, and clothing. When God's people have more than they need, they face another temptation that is just as debilitating. When Jesus resisted the devil in His temptation experience, He quoted Deuteronomy 8:3. This narrative reveals the critical danger of having an abundance of provisions that cannot be ignored.

Since Jesus quoted this event in Israel's history to deal with His temptation experience, it also proved relevant on how Jesus taught

His men how to pray. The better part of practical wisdom would follow the Lord's logic on why He connected these narratives when He taught His men to ask their heavenly Father for daily bread.

THE PERIL OF AFFLUENCE

Moses commanded Israel that their highest priority was to be obedient to the Lord, especially as He led them into the land He promised to their forefathers. He reminded them how God led them through the wilderness for forty years to humble them and test them to see what was in their heart. *He let them go hungry and provided manna to teach them that they do not live by bread alone but by every word that proceeds from the mouth of God in Deuteronomy 8:2-3.* All their need for food, clothing, and shelter was provided. This wilderness was not luxury, but their needs were provided.

The Promised Land was a place where they would lack nothing (Deuteronomy 8:9). They would have more than they needed, and they would be abundantly satisfied. The proper response was to bless the Lord their God for what He had given to them (Deuteronomy 8:10). The temptation was clear. The danger of being filled and having an abundance was to forget about God and stop obeying His commands. Nothing captured this better than Moses's warning to Israel in Deuteronomy 8:11-14 (NASB1995):

> "Beware that you do not forget the Lord your God by not keeping His commandments and His ordinances and His statutes which I am commanding you today; otherwise, when you have eaten and are satisfied, and have built good houses and lived in them, and when your herds and your flocks multiply, and your silver and gold multiply, and all that you have multiplies, then your heart will become proud and you will forget the Lord your God who brought you out from the land of Egypt, out of the house of slavery."

The danger was exacerbated when His people fell victim to this self-deception. Moses warned Israel to guard themselves from thinking it was by their own power and strength that made all this wealth when it was God who was giving them the strength to build this wealth (Deuteronomy 8:17-18). Moses's final warning was if they ever forgot God and worshiped other gods, they would certainly perish.

Asking the Father to provide for daily bread expresses a sense of divine appreciation for God's generous provision for life. It is intended to avoid two dangerous pitfalls: having too little makes everyone vulnerable to Satan's deception, and personal needs take precedence over God's purpose. The second danger is having too much and allowing arrogance to reduce God to an irrelevant symbol. The problem is developing a "god complex" where we reject the generosity of the Father, convinced we are masters of our own fate and, by our own strength, have all these things.

When people are deprived of basic needs, they either give up or do unimaginable things. Everyone is capable of ill-conceived wrongdoing when they are struggling, especially regarding their needs. People will do illegal things when they get desperate. The devil has the perfect leverage to manipulate God's people into losing confidence in their heavenly Father and trusting themselves.

The possibility of failure is sobering. A child of God may understand his or her identity as a child of God, pray earnestly for God's kingdom to come, and desire for His will to be done on earth as God envisions it in heaven. They may even have a keen sense of His holiness and a conviction that they are to treat God as holy.

Children of God may also have a strong sense of God's forgiveness and the responsibility to forgive others. We may believe in the value of eternal things and focus clearly on the power of our Father's presence. But the pivot point to move beyond these things is completely dependent on having a kind of faith that rests fully on His provision. There is no greater distraction to an abundant and full relationship with the Father than anxiety.

All that being said, the vitality of the life of a child of God may be rendered inert and ineffective because he or she does not understand how to live in dependence on his or her heavenly Father. Our prayer ought to ask our heavenly Father to guard our hearts from taking Him for granted. Nothing could be more disrespectful to the Lord than for His children to think they do not need Him, especially on a daily basis.

The words of Agur, the son of Jakeh, may best capture Jesus' heartbeat regarding this portion of His prayer. It also arrests our own heart to understand the critical nature of asking our heavenly Father to provide for our daily bread:

Remove far from me falsehood and lying; give me neither poverty nor riches; feed me with the food that is needful for me, lest I be full and deny you and say, "Who is the LORD?" or lest I be poor and steal and profane the name of my God (Proverbs 30:8-9).

Nothing will put God's children on the sidelines quicker than being consumed with anxiety because we simply cannot trust that God will provide. The other pitfall is deciding we do not need Him anymore because we have an abundance of resources and become arrogant toward His gracious provision. The benefits of trusting our heavenly Father to provide everything we need to shape the way we live is far more important than demanding He must protect our way of life.

PRINCIPLES IN TRUSTING GOD TO PROVIDE DAILY BREAD:

1. Asking God to provide daily bread requires a unique commitment of faith.

   - What areas in your life make you the most vulnerable to temptation?
   - To what extent do you take God for granted? How do you keep from being indifferent to Him because you don't need him?

2. The evidence of genuine faith in God's daily provision will be seen by a lack of anxiety in one's life. Conversely, anxiety undermines faith.

   - How would you describe how anxiety afflicts your life? What do you believe is the primary reason for these experiences?
   - What have you done to deal with moments of anxiety in your life? How much has your relationship with the Lord helped?

3. Instead of spending all of our lives stockpiling earthly goods, Christ calls us to seek God's kingdom and His righteousness.

   - How do you invest your time and resources for God's kingdom?
   - How do your actions reflect your commitment to storing up treasures in heaven?

4. Anxiety and worry usually separate our core values and focus from seeking first His kingdom and righteousness to being consumed with first-world concerns.

   - When do you feel divided in your relationship with your heavenly Father and your own priorities?

- What impact has a lack of focus had on your relationship with Christ?

PRAYER

Lord, nothing has been more debilitating in my own life than anxiety and worry. Help me to understand that faith is a critical element in abating worry in my life. Help me to trust you because your care for me goes far beyond your care for your creation.

I acknowledge that the greatest evidence of not allowing anxiety to infiltrate my life is my commitment to seeking after your kingdom work here on earth and to living according to your righteousness. I want to prioritize my life to invest in your kingdom. Help me demonstrate uncommon faith and rely on you for the basic needs of life.

We ask all these things in Jesus's strong name, Amen.

CHAPTER 5

UNFORGIVENESS IS TOXIC

Why Holding Grudges
Isn't Worth It

"Forgive us our debts, as we forgive our debtors."

Matthew 6:12

D o not judge, lest you be judged. For in the way you judge, you will be judged; and by your standard of measure, it will be measured to you. And why do you look at the speck that is in your brother's eye, but do not notice the log that is in your own eye? Or how can you say to your brother, Let me take the speck out of your eye, and behold, the log in our own eye? You hypocrite first take the log out of your own eye, and then you will see clearly to take the speck out of your brother's eye.

Do not give what is holy to dogs, and do not throw your pearls before pigs, or they will trample them under their feet, and turn and tear you to pieces. Matthew 7:1-6, NASB

I grew up in a pretty stable home. My mom was a believer, and my dad was a moralist. Together, my parents provided a solid family unit that created a pretty healthy household. They were both active and intentional about being involved in our lives. They provided some great support for their three sons.

However, due to my insecurities and broken self-worth, I spent much of my life trying to get my dad's approval. I desperately wanted my dad to be proud of me, but no matter how hard I tried, I never thought he gave it to me. This battle caused some deep-rooted anxiety in my spirit that drove me to embrace a performance-driven sense of self-worth and significance.

When I hit college, I read through a book called *Inside Out* by Lawrence Crabb. It was here that I finally came to grips with forgiving my dad for not giving me what I felt I needed from him. I bawled my eyes out for over half an hour. The transformation was almost instantaneous. I suddenly found freedom from my frustration towards my dad, who had driven and defined my life for years. Of course, when I finally forgave my dad, I also came to the realization that only God could fill the critical needs in my life related to self-worth, significance, and security. My dad was not as bad as I thought he was.

THE FORGIVENESS OF THE FATHER

One of the most potent aspects of the Lord's Prayer revolves around forgiveness. Jesus knew that living in a broken and sinful world would be impossible without needing to forgive others for their behavior. Learning to forgive is an essential part of understanding one's relationship with our heavenly Father and operating in a sinful world.

This element alone was absolutely critical. Jesus mentioned this element in the prayer, using forgiveness to explain the essential nature of God being their heavenly Father and then expounding on how indispensable this characteristic is in His kingdom work here on earth.

This segment of the Lord's Prayer expresses a contingency for God to forgive His children's debts as we forgive our debtors. This connects our choices towards others with our heavenly Father. How we treat others impacts our relationship with God, and how we respond to God impacts our human relationships.

Forgiving debts can simply refer to money owed to someone else. Luke, a parallel text, describes the need to forgive "sins" (Luke 11:4). Matthew broadens the range of meaning when he also writes about forgiving "transgressions" (Matthew 6:14-15).

Even if this petition only refers to financial debts, very few things create more dissent and conflict in relationships than issues surrounding money. However, the overriding principle is that the Father calls His children to forgive others regardless of the issue because God has forgiven us; forgiving others is imperative because this is the Father's character and generous provision to His children.

Since the Father's forgiveness is about much deeper issues than simply financial debts, it would stand to reason that the spirit of Jesus's teaching expected His disciples to forgive others for the same issues that the Father had forgiven them. Since sin and evil plague the hearts of everyone, in the same way the Father forgave us, we should, in turn, forgive others who also manifest the same or similar sin and evil towards us. No matter how sinful or evil a person is toward us, we can rest assured that the Father's forgiveness goes deeper.

To understand Jesus's mindset, we must remember that there are actually two sides to the issue of forgiveness. This may not seem obvious at first, but it is definitely present. He commanded His disciples to forgive others because their Father had forgiven them, but the opposite is also true. Forgiveness is still a choice of obedience, just as much as choosing not to forgive is a choice of disobedience.

The real warning here is about an unforgiving heart. The context of the Lord's Prayer is about family fellowship, not salvation, as we typically think about it. While it would be impossible to avoid all conflict in relationships, it is important to learn how to forgive because it is vital to a healthy family relationship. The potential danger when others sin against us is being wounded so deeply that holding an unforgiving attitude is a very real danger.

Being a victim of others' sin can become the breeding ground for animosity. The pain of betrayal can empower unforgiveness and tempt anyone to attempt to carry out their own justice. But when there is no clear pathway for perceived justice, the danger of developing an unforgiving spirit becomes a real attraction.

Unforgiveness is inconsistent with honoring their Father. How we treat others, especially when we are wrongfully treated, is of utmost importance to our Father. An unwillingness to forgive indicates a failure to learn how to imitate the forgiveness He shows us. The problem of unforgiveness can only be seen when we listen to Jesus's explanation in Matthew 7:1-6.

THE DANGER OF UNFORGIVENESS

As a pastor, I often find myself in a counseling role. Over years of ministry, I have had numerous conversations with individuals who had been insulted, offended, or hurt by another. Regardless if it is criticizing them or there is moral failure, they struggle to know how to proceed.

The hurt and pain are always overwhelming, and the struggle to know the right thing to do is often confusing. They are dealing with a barrage of emotions: anger, bitterness, extreme sadness, discouragement, even depression. There is always a desire for justice, but in the chaos of betrayal, it often seems an impossible venture. The emotional battle is a perfect storm that throws whole families into a turmoil of confusion and disappointment. But this is not the only struggle.

On top of the emotional struggle, individuals flounder, trying to grasp the Biblical responsibility to navigate the turmoil that devastates their lives. In spite of how long many of them had been walking with the Lord, there is often as much confusion related to their next Biblical step due to the emotional confusion inside of them. The issue is not that they did not know what the Bible teaches. The issue is whether they are going to obey what God wants them to do, and it is never a foregone conclusion. But few realize how this battle can put them in even greater danger.

Everyone generally agrees that there are real dangers every believer will inevitably face in the world. We often underestimate those things that appear harmless, but these very things often become greater threats. John warned believers of the typical evils every believer needs to address: the lust of the eyes, the lust of the flesh, and the boastful pride of life (1 John 2:16). Theologically, there is general agreement on these fundamental challenges believers will face: the world, the flesh, and Satan.

It is hard to imagine a more serious threat to the well-being of God's people and God's kingdom work. But in reality, Jesus pointed out in the Lord's Prayer that there is an even greater threat than these things; it is the toxic infection of unforgiveness.

When the Father is faced with one of His own who refuses to forgive, as any good Father would, He must confront and discipline His child to teach them what it means to belong to His family. When God's people grieve His Spirit by not forgiving each other, He actively seeks to bring them to a point of repentance so they can eagerly engage according to His power and righteousness.

In Matthew 7:1-12, Jesus gives more details to help His men understand the nature of forgiveness. But he began, not by addressing the principle of forgiveness, but by explaining the danger of unforgiveness:

> "Do not judge, lest you be judged. For in the way you judge, you will be judged; and by your standard of measure, it will be measured to you. And why do you look at the speck that is in your brother's eye, but do not notice the log that is in your own eye? Or how can you say to your brother, Let me take the speck out of your eye, and behold, the log in our own eye? You hypocrite first take the log out of your own eye, and then you will see clearly to take the speck out of your brother's eye. "Do not give dogs what is holy, and do not throw your pearls before pigs, lest they trample them underfoot and turn to attack you."
>
> Matthew 7:1-6, NASB 1977

THE DANGER OF JUDGMENTALISM

As we put ourselves in the disciple's shoes, Jesus taught that an unwillingness to forgive others results in judgmentalism (Matthew 7:1-2). When someone was sinned against, the victim had three choices: They could try to ignore and forget the offense, they could forgive them, or they could react by judging the person who broke trust with them.

When bad things happen to someone, our hearts cry out for justice. If they don't believe justice will occur, the temptation to become judge and jury is undeniable. Judgmentalism typically manifests itself with criticism, gossip, condemnation, and even slander.

In extreme pain, even personal attacks on someone's character are common.

Jesus warned His disciples that when someone judges another person, that person often judges them. This reciprocal action is inevitable, where one seeks justice and the other defends themselves. Judgment is quick and not quiet. One attack leads to a counterattack to defend and take revenge on the person who started this battle. Retaliation is often a means to protect and to get even. Unfortunately, these strategies usually escalate the animosity between individuals, and if someone does not stand down, the process continues to deteriorate.

With a skillful play on words, Jesus taught that the measure or standard by which we judge others will be the measure by which we are judged (Matthew 7:1-2). People pass judgment rather than have conversations. People do not necessarily want to reconcile; they want to win. Everyone has certain standards or expectations of how people should behave and treat others based on how they desire to be treated, regardless of whether they are conscious of those demands or not.

Due to the contingency that God forgives as His people forgive others, then the reverse is true, too. If His people refuse to forgive others, then God will not forgive them. In fact, God makes a judgment on His children when they refuse to do what He has asked them to do. He does it with perfect love and righteousness. Because He delights in His children, He will exhort them to act in a manner that reflects His character. In other words, the motivation to forgive others is always grounded in God's forgiveness for His people.

THE DANGER WHEN UNFORGIVENESS BECOMES NORMAL

Everyone hates the feeling when someone gets away with an injustice. *Forgiveness protects the offender from the victim attempting to enforce their own justice or revenge.* Forgiveness also protects the one victimized from becoming deeply entangled in their anger and giving control of their life to the pain of offense. Forgiveness brings freedom by entrusting the offense to the heavenly Father, who will bring about true justice according to His own righteousness and divine purpose.

Forgiveness also frees the victim from spiritual idolatry. Unresolved anger and pain will poison the heart and give control to the person who sinned against them. Unforgiveness results in wrapping one's life around one's anger towards the one who sinned against them. Their life is no longer shaped by faith in their heavenly Father but by fear and the person who hurt them. One does not find emotional healing in order to forgive as much as forgiveness opens the door for personal healing.

> "And why do you look at the speck that is in your brother's eye, but do not notice the log that is in your own eye? Or how can you say to your brother, Let me take the speck out of your eye, and behold, the log in our own eye?"
>
> Matthew 7:3-4, NASB1977

Jesus now expands the focus of His teaching while introducing another level of collateral damage from unforgiveness. Taking the speck out of someone's eye is an idiomatic expression about seeing and pointing out the shortcomings and problems in others. The mood of the text transitions from direct judgment of those who sin to fault-finding towards others who are part of the larger community of believers.

The repeated reference in these verses to "your brother" indicates that the primary audience is still God's people. The "log" is an intentionally ludicrous exaggeration of personal issues in contrast to the speck of sawdust in another's life. What is a tiny flaw in another is seen so clearly by a critical person, while ironically, what is an outrageously huge failure in the latter is conveniently overlooked altogether. It is the self-righteous, censorious person who is particularly eager to correct the faults of others.[8]

> "You hypocrite, first take the log out of your own eye, and then you will see clearly to take the speck out of your brother's eye."
>
> Matthew 7:5

First, it is important to note what Jesus is not saying. He is not advocating that His children start comparing their problems with the faults in others and if they determine that their own faults were less significant than a brother or sister, this gives permission to point out their faults. There was no latitude in this context that *taking the speck out of my brother's eye* has any positive or redeeming attributes.

Humans, and especially believers, are notorious for mitigating personal issues and magnifying the problems of others, which is, in fact, the problem in this text. What often is judged as a character issue in other people's lives is excused as circumstantial in one's own life. But this new pattern of being overly critical towards others is not just the residual effect of having a bad day; it is driven by the primary problem of having unresolved unforgiveness in the heart.

COMPARING SPECKS AND LOGS

Jesus taught that when a person has a "log" in their own eye, that must take precedence over issues in anyone else's life. Most com-

---

8 Hagner, Donald A. *Matthew 1-13*. Vol. 33A, Word Biblical Commentary, Word, 1993.

mentaries often point out that this is not saying we can never speak into another person's life, but that everyone must always deal with their own issues before ever taking a look at the issues of others. But that actually misses the point of what Jesus is teaching in this text.

In this case, Jesus assumed that the log in our own eye is the primary problem in this narrative, not the speck in someone else's eye. Jesus is not advocating that His disciples need to address the log in their own eye so they can properly deal with the specks in the lives of others. He advocated dealing with the log in their own eye so that they will not become fixated on the issues in others by ignoring the key problems in their own lives.

This "log" in their own eye is not just any kind of sin. The logic of Jesus's argument points to the fact that the log is a spirit of unforgiveness. The collateral damage of unforgiveness produces a toxic and censorious attitude that feels entitled to find fault with everyone around them – first the person who sinned against them and then of those in the general community. This log of unforgiveness *always* trumps any speck in someone else's eye because a spirit that has been poisoned by unforgiveness can never see anyone's life from the perspective of their heavenly Father, much less their own.

Jesus condemned this hypocrisy, and rightly so. The solution may seem obvious, but Jesus is speaking to a deeper issue. The only apparent basis for taking the speck out of someone else's eye is to deal with the log in one's own eye. But the solution solves itself. Since the motivation to focus on the smallest of issues in someone's life is driven by a spirit of unforgiveness, then the moment someone deals with the "log," in their own eye, an unforgiving attitude, the specks in other people's lives become inconsequential.

Once unforgiveness has been resolved, then the collateral effects of that disappear too. There is no need to keep on judging others when a believer truly forgives. There is no longer any purpose pointing out other people's faults when a person forgives because the toxic anger of unforgiveness is resolved too. The anger disappears and the need to channel that anger towards finding faults in others becomes a non-issue. It is the perfect pathway to humility.

THE GREATEST DANGER OF UNFORGIVENESS

"Do not give dogs what is holy, and do not throw your pearls before pigs, lest they trample them underfoot and turn to attack you."

Matthew 7:6

I remember that for my first classes at Southern Institute for Technology, I enrolled in the civil engineering program, and one of the classes was calculus. The introduction class was mind-boggling and it almost convinced me to quit. The language and complexity of calculus was like a foreign language to me. The teacher could say the same things a dozen times, but it still made no sense.

Fortunately, we had an amazing professor who made even the demands of this discipline seem pretty straightforward. I certainly did not finish at the top of the class, but I did pass the course. The key to everything was having a professor who was meticulous in explaining how we were to think through the nature of this discipline. If it wasn't for him, I never would have figured it out on my own.

Possibly, the most enigmatic verse in all the Scriptures is Matthew 7:6. Some commentators have simply surrendered to the dilemma that there is no feasible way to make sense of Jesus's statement. Others have warned to not build any doctrine or even principles based on this saying because of the difficulty interpreting the idiomatic nature of Jesus's expression. It appears to make little sense in the immediate context and does not fit anything even in the larger context.

However, Jesus did include this strange statement in what He taught, so our assumption is that it had a very strategic purpose. He included it for some reason, even if it appears to evade our understanding. The Spirit of God deemed it necessary for Matthew to include it in the narrative. To miss how Jesus intended this to fit would seem to be disappointing at the very least.

Most agree, as a starting point, that pearls and holy things refer to things which have great value. In the eyes of Jesus, and certainly the Father, whatever is holy is valuable because Jesus declared it to be something of great value. In the same way, pearls are also something of great value, even if we do not know what this means at this moment. It is very clear Jesus is warning His disciples against doing something inappropriate with things that Jesus deems to be of great value.

Dogs and pigs are generally considered metaphorical references to people who are non-Jews or unbelievers who are outside God's community (Matthew 15:26; Philippians 3:2; Revelations 22:15). They are not part of God's family and do not understand His will or purpose.

Consequently, Christ warns the disciples that there are some who will be antagonistic towards those things that are holy, and they may turn on God's people too. Some have proposed that "what is holy" refers to God's people, or, in this case, followers of Christ.

This suggestion reflects the wisdom of Proverbs, warning us to avoid the wicked because of the imminent danger to oneself (Proverbs 1:10-19; 4:14-19). While that has some Biblical merit, it would appear that pearls and holy things are something distinct from the people who "throw them before the dogs and pigs".

But the warning is disturbing. These antagonists not only trample on things of great value but also tear to pieces those who share those things. Their response appears to be unmatched hostility with extreme prejudice. But unless we can interpret what Jesus intended, we end up making inductive guesses as to the purpose of His statements.

The most common interpretation of what is holy is the gospel. If anything is holy, it is the message of good news of the kingdom of God (Matthew 4:23). This interpretation proposes that Jesus warned His men to be careful with whom they share the gospel. If it is obvious that their audience was hard-hearted and hostile to their message, He gave them permission to not share that which is holy because all that would do would invite their wrath.

There are examples of Jesus telling the disciples not to keep on sharing the message of the kingdom. When He sent His disciples to the lost house of Israel, if they were received by the residents of any city, they would stay and share their message. If they were not received, they were to shake the dust off their sandals and leave (Matthew 10:14; Mark 6:11; Luke 9:5).

Jesus went on to say that it would be more tolerable for Sodom and Gomorrah on the day of judgment than for these cities that did not receive His disciples (Matthew 10:15). But all this referred to their judgment for rejecting the message, not necessarily for inferring hostility towards the disciples. The biggest problem with this interpretation is the context.

Matthew 7:1-6 warned against judging others and pointing out the flaws in others, followed by Jesus's condemnation of such hypocrisy. Jesus is condemning the behavior of those who experience forgiveness from the Father but refuse to forgive others. The only way to conclude that holy things is now referring to the gospel is if one deliberately removes this verse from the context Jesus placed it within. That which is holy must refer to something other than the gospel or God's people.

To understand this verse, we must go back to one of the most important principles of interpretation, which is the principle of context. The sequence of Jesus's thought process is absolutely critical to see how Jesus interpreted these first six verses related to His prayer.

THE UNPARALLELED DAMAGE OF UNFORGIVENESS

Jesus taught the priority of forgiveness (Matthew 6:7-12). His interpretation of that prayer warned His men first about the dangers of unforgiveness (Matthew 7:1-6). Unforgiveness resulted in judging those who sinned against them. Inevitably, the toxic nature of unforgiveness would eventually turn to an attitude of criticism, which will spread to include others in the community (Matthew 7:3-4). Jesus called these people out for their hypocrisy. The log that needed to be removed from their eye was specifically an unforgiving spirit. This was the source of all this negative behavior in this particular context. Unless this problem was addressed, the ensuing collateral damage would continue to pile up.

There is no reason to think that Jesus suddenly changed direction and abandoned this line of thought when He gets to verse six. In fact, we will discover that verse six is Jesus's most stringent warning to His disciples about the enormous dangers of an unforgiving attitude.

The truth we discover in the greater context of the Lord's Prayer is that the one thing that is explicitly referred to as holy is God's name (Matthew 6:9). Jesus taught His men that to pray "hallowed be your name" says more about their responsibility to God then what God should be and do for them.

God is holy because this is part of His nature. He does not need anyone or anything to make Him holy. But their prayer would infer that the disciples needed to live in such a manner so that they would always treat God as holy. They would behave in such a way that God would be pleased with their behavior, and people would see the profound reverence and respect they had for their heavenly Father by the way they lived.

Therefore, what Jesus taught in Matthew 7:6, in light of the context of His prayer, we are not to take God's holy name and give it to dogs. But Jesus is not advocating we should stop sharing the good news of the gospel. He is saying that we should not act in such a way that dishonors God's name in front of unbelievers. This is not a new concern. It was a concern the Lord had with Israel all through the Old Testament, as we see in Ezekiel 36:22-23:

> "Therefore say to the house of Israel, 'Thus says the Lord God, "It is not for your sake, O house of Israel, that I am about to act, but for My holy name, which you have profaned among the nations where you went. I will vindicate the holiness of My great name which has been profaned among the nations, which you have profaned in their midst. Then the nations will know that I am the Lord," declares the Lord God, "when I prove Myself holy among you in their sight."

Israel blasphemed God's name by their disobedience and sin. They had defiled the Land, and God's wrath was upon them. He exiled them to the nations, and they were mocked by these foreigners, who were astonished. These are the people of the Lord, yet they were now exiles (Ezekial 36:16-20).

Jesus's warning to "not give what is holy to dogs" would be better translated as "do not throw or blaspheme God's holy name before unbelievers." In our cultural slang, it would be "don't throw God under a bus." This warning is emphatically **not** about giving a gift that is rejected. This warned of the danger of an unforgiving spirit and the incalculable damage it can do by creating a deeply embedded hypocrisy of unforgiveness, reflected by attitude and actions that blaspheme God's holy name and undermine His credibility in the world.

DISHONORING GOD'S HOLY NAME BEFORE UNBELIEVERS

When unbelievers experience a follower of Jesus operating out of unforgiveness, they run into a child of God separated from their fellowship with their heavenly Father. Their life is marked by grumbling, complaining, criticism, and judgmentalism. They whine about other believers who did them wrong. They regularly find things wrong in other believers, and they are unashamed to complain even in front of unbelievers.

In our context, a person with unforgiveness complains more about the "specs" in other believers, the hypocrisy of leadership, and the problems of the institutionalized church than seeing their own. *When a believer lives with the toxic poison of unforgiveness for any length of time, a complaining spirit becomes normal around everyone, about everyone, even in front of unbelievers.*

But if that is not sobering enough, Jesus points out that the collateral damage of unforgiveness can get even worse. Unforgiveness not only destroys human relationships but also deteriorates our relationship with our Heavenly Father and His kingdom work here on earth.

Jesus warned His men to not throw pearls before swine. Nothing in the Lord's Prayer itself, nor in Jesus's explanation to this point, talks about pearls. The only other reference in Matthew to a pearl of any kind is Matthew 13:45-46: "Again, the kingdom of heaven is like a merchant seeking fine pearls, and upon finding one pearl of great value, he went and sold all that he had and bought it (NASB1995)."

This parable is about comparing the kingdom of heaven to a pearl of great price. The truth here is that when a merchant found this rare pearl, he realized it was priceless, and he immediately sold everything he owned just to obtain it. While there is much that we could observe here, the one critical element of this parable is the picture of a pearl is directly connected to the kingdom of heaven. The other observation, as far as Jesus was concerned, is that the kingdom of heaven is intrinsically valuable and very important to the heart of Jesus.

Jesus introduced the kingdom of heaven to His men at the very outset of teaching them to pray. Their Father, who dwells in the heavens, has a kingdom that is coming, and His will is to be done on earth as God purposed in heaven.

When we circle back to Matthew 7:6, we can identify that the reference to a pearl has to be related to the kingdom of heaven to be consistent with how Matthew used this term. The Father's kingdom is the pearl Jesus referred to in this verse. We also need to notice that "pearl" is grammatically plural. Therefore, there are at least two pearls that Jesus referred to when He charged His disciples to not throw or cast them before unbelievers. We know the first has to do with the kingdom of heaven. The second is hidden in plain sight.

The closest reference to the kingdom of heaven to Matthew 7:6 happens to be a few verses back in Matthew 6:33, and there is value in including the previous verse for context:

"For the Gentiles seek after all these things, and your heavenly Father knows that you need them all. But seek first the kingdom of God and his righteousness, and all these things will be added to you."

Matthew 6:32-33

While the Gentiles eagerly pursued all these things (food, shelter, clothing) and stockpiled them as a measure of self-worth, significance, and success, Jesus commanded His disciples to keep on seeking two things: the kingdom of God and His righteousness. These are the two pearls that were most precious to Jesus and certainly treasured by our heavenly Father. The warning of Matthew 7:6 is that a believer can undermine God's kingdom work and His claim to be a righteous God by the hypocrisy of an unforgiving spirit.

The disciples' measure of significance and success was their commitment to God's kingdom and upholding His righteousness. Jesus taught His men that, in the likeness of not throwing what is holy to dogs, they should not throw these pearls before swine. The force of throwing or casting captures the intensity of His concern in much the same way as it relates to not giving what is holy to dogs.

PEARLS AND PIGS

When followers of Jesus allow unforgiveness to dominate their lives, they lose sight of how valuable these things are to the heart of the Father. Through hypocritical behavior, they cast these precious things before unbelievers like they have no value at all.

Consequently, when a child of God allows the toxic waste of unforgiveness into their relationships, especially towards unbelievers, they not only blaspheme God's holy name, but they also discredit God's kingdom and His righteousness here on earth.

In order to relate to this, in our new covenant relationship with Christ, God's kingdom work is the church. Christ redeemed men and women to be in a vital relationship with Him and the Father to carry out His redemptive kingdom work here on earth by living according to His will. Much of that will center around the gospel of Jesus.

God is holy and righteous. Since He is willing to forgive us of our sin, transgression, and spiritual debt, He calls us to be holy and live righteously in this world. The way we honor our heavenly Father and treat Him as holy means living in a manner that prioritizes His kingdom, seeking His righteousness, and doing His will. At the top of the list in how we honor our Father is learning to forgive.

One of the unfortunate perceptions unbelievers have of the church is often a list of complicated and distasteful issues. There are truly abominable things that have given the world a reason to reject the church and the God we serve. Cases of sexual immorality, fraud, abuse of ecclesiastical power, and abuse of women and children all border on the unforgivable, at least from a human perspective.

These are also things that have caused many Christians to abandon the church and find their own way apart from organized religion. While there may appear to be many reasons for the world to reject God, the church, and their claim to righteousness, one must wonder how much unforgiveness has been the deep-seated, toxic core for the manifestation of these evils that have destroyed the lives of believers and decimated God's kingdom work on earth.

Jesus's final statement in verse six now makes sense. This particular hypocrisy not only catches the anger of unbelievers, but they project that anger toward God and also those two key pearls He values above all else: His kingdom work and doing His will. His kingdom work is to be carried out by the church and everything that can be encompassed by His righteousness.

ONE REASON THE WORLD HATES CHRISTIANS

The duplicity of unforgiveness is absolutely catastrophic. Jesus was not suggesting in this verse that believers were persecuted as martyrs because of the gospel. He warned His disciples in the strongest possible language that when the toxic spirit of unforgiveness is seen by an unbelieving world, "they will trample these precious pearls of His kingdom and His righteousness underfoot, and then turn and attack you."

The lesson is somewhat self-evident. No believer can afford to carry a spirit of unforgiveness; it simply is too dangerous in every sense of the word. It clearly does not reflect the Father's heart or His kindness to forgive His children. But the collateral damage to relationships is endless. Unforgiveness destroys the unity of the Body, and when unbelievers experience the corrupted spirit of a believer's unforgiveness, they blaspheme God's holy name. Even unbelievers cannot tolerate or excuse this kind of hypocrisy. In fact, they long to point out the uselessness of the church and any claim to serving a righteous God because if this is the result in the life of one of Christ's followers, they want nothing to do with it.

HOW DOES ONE FIND FREEDOM FROM UNFORGIVENESS

There has been an ongoing dispute that one must emotionally heal before they can forgive or they must forgive in order to emotionally heal. The better part of Jesus's wisdom in Matthew 7:1-6 clearly indicates how dangerous unforgiveness can become in any of His followers. The pathway of unforgiveness will always become more toxic over time, not less. Time does not always heal, and when it comes to an unforgiving spirit, it is impossible to experience complete healing and freedom unless one forgives; that is the mandate of His prayer.

The admonition of the Lord's Prayer is that God's children are to forgive as He has forgiven them. There is always the temptation to brush off minor offenses, disregard insults, and pretend the actions of others did not really hurt us. However, regardless of whether the offense is big or small, the result of an unforgiving spirit is a life shaped by anger and bitterness that continually pours into the lives of those around us.

The risk one takes with any form of offense is that one is wounded far more significantly than they are willing to admit. When left unresolved, the emotional and relational toll continues to build over time, and everything believers hold precious can be carelessly placed in harm's way. Too many Christians are walking around still bitter about things that happened to them years ago, and these past experiences will continue to damage their own life if they choose not to forgive. This is the most severe warning Jesus gave to His disciples because there are fewer things more dangerous to everyone and God's kingdom work than an unforgiving spirit.

PRINCIPLES OF THE DANGER OF UNFORGIVENESS:

1. Forgiveness is the one kingdom responsibility that always affects two relationships: our relationship with another human and our relationship with our heavenly Father.

   - How much has the actions of others impacted your relationship with your heavenly Father?
   - Is there someone in your life you need to forgive?

2. Unforgiveness is one of the most dangerous spiritual diseases that can infect a Christian. It will destroy personal relationships and the community of faith.

   - Do you have people in your life that you avoid or refuse to talk with because there is some unresolved issue between you and them?
   - How has unforgiveness adversely affected relationships in your life?

3. Jesus's most stringent warning is to show that the toxic nature of forgiveness can cause a person to blaspheme God's name, destroy His kingdom work, and undermine any claim the church has on righteousness.

   - What is your reputation amongst your unbelieving friends at school, work, or neighborhood?
   - What is the nature of your spiritual conversations with unbelievers? Do you celebrate the Lord and His church or do you complain about these things in front of unbelievers?

PRAYER

Heavenly Father, I recognize that there are segments of my life that I have ignored for years, seeking to control or manage hurt by others. I realize these things are like spiritual sewage in my spirit, and I ask you to forgive me for not forgiving others. Today, I will take time to discover those who I have not forgiven, and I will honor you by choosing to forgive those who I have not forgiven.

Please create in me a clean heart and renew a new spirit in me. I realize that I have dishonored you and not treated you as my holy, heavenly Father who has forgiven me of much deeper evils than what you are asking me to forgive of others. In Christ's Name, Amen.

CHAPTER 6

FORGIVENESS IS A SUPERPOWER

Freeing Yourself from Others Through Grace

"And forgive us our debts, as we forgive our debtors."

Matthew 6:12

"Ask, and it shall be given to you; seek, and you shall find; knock, and it shall be opened to you. For everyone who asks receives, and he who seeks finds, and to him who knocks it shall be opened. Or what man is there among you, when his son shall ask him for a loaf, will give him a stone? Or if he shall ask for a fish, he will not give him a snake, will he? If then you then, being evil, know how to give good gifts to your children, how much more shall your Father who is in heaven give what is good to those who ask Him! Therefore, however you want people to treat you, so treat them, for this is the Law and the Prophets."

Matthew 7:7-12, NASB1977

"Failure is not an option." This could have been my motto growing up. I had a very broken self-image and needed acceptance from everyone. I had succumbed to a perfectionistic model of significance in an effort to gain my dad's approval. I not only had to do everything with excellence, but if anyone ever found anything wrong with anything that I did, I considered my efforts as a failure. No matter how hard I tried, I felt my dad kept withholding his approval, which, in turn, deepened my anger towards him and even more so towards myself. Only when I was better than everyone did I feel like an equal.

The struggle to avoid this feeling of worthlessness was overwhelming. If I played table games with family and friends, it felt like a life-and-death battle. I had to win just to feel valuable. If I had any inclination that someone else might beat me at the game, I would deliberately start losing just so they could not say they beat me. Maintaining some sense of personal self-worth was exhausting and debilitating. The most tortuous dilemma in all of this was seeing no way out of this worthlessness and failure. It was only when I discovered God's healing that I found freedom from both unforgiveness and feelings of personal worthlessness.

One of the most devastating realities for a child of God is moral failure. Failure fueled by the toxic waste of unforgiveness is a moral failure as damaging as any other. We cannot ignore the fact that Matthew 7:7-12 follows one of the most severe warnings in all of the Scriptures. When the hypocrisy of unforgiveness has made a mess of one's reputation, allowing that bitterness to damage other relationships and dishonor one's heavenly Father, the depths of failure are unmatched. However, even under these circumstances, God continues to provide a redemption pathway. Jesus made that same truth very clear in this text too.

DEALING WITH FAILURE

Two Biblical characters create an interesting picture of dealing with failure: Judas and Peter. Judas betrayed Christ and delivered Him to the Pharisees and Scribes. When he finally realized the depth of his betrayal, he disposed of the money and hung himself. His failure was so utterly overwhelming that he was convinced it was unforgivable.

Peter also failed miserably when he blatantly denied knowing Jesus on three different occasions the night Judas betrayed Him. In spite of previously confronting Jesus when He announced His suffering and death, Peter adamantly said he would stand with Jesus even if it meant his own death. The Biblical record shows how easily he stumbled to his own humiliation. The third time he denied Jesus, Jesus turned and looked directly at him, and he went out and wept bitterly (Luke 22:61-62).

These verses offer a twofold purpose of how we are to step back into Christ's narrative. The text gives us God's instructions to help us in dealing with our own failure of hypocrisy. Secondly, when we are willing to live with the consequences of other people's bad behavior by forgiving them, this text also helps us understand how God is willing to stand in the gap for us. It is important to see both the immediate context and the larger picture of Jesus's exposition related to His prayer.

This threefold description of asking, seeking, and knocking is about finding forgiveness and healing for the failure of unforgiveness. These three verbal ideas of ask, seek, and knock are all commands, but none of them have direct objects. Jesus did not designate to whom these activities are directed. This is important as He finished off His teaching about the dangers of unforgiveness. These truths are just as critical.

The Christian community has used these three activities as a general formula for seeking the Lord and a method of prayer. The encouragement has often been on persistence in prayer and seeking the Lord. There are often no boundaries that establish the nature of this kind of prayer and no context for discerning the purpose of this threefold admonition. These have simply become a formula of how to address almost any issue or circumstance needing divine help.

That being said, the application has jumped in front of interpretation. Because these verses are rarely seen in context, mostly because of the lingering ambiguity of the text, they are treated as independent ideas and, therefore, understood as a universal principle related to prayer.

UNDERSTANDING TRUE FORGIVENESS

But since Matthew 7:6 can now be understood as one of the most severe warnings Jesus ever spoke about the hypocrisy and collateral damage of unforgiveness, this context may provide a more precise interpretation.

There is an obvious shift in tone from verse six to verse seven. For the sake of context, when a child of God suddenly realizes that unforgiveness has become so toxic in their own heart that they have become an infamous example of verse one through six, they realize they have damaged several relationships, hurt a number of other believers, and even spewed their bitterness among unbelievers, they are face to face with their own moral and spiritual failure. Regardless of the extent, a person who is convinced that they have blasphemed God's holy name, undermined God's kingdom work, and abandoned a life reflecting His righteousness desperately needs forgiveness.

The utter horror and magnitude of this kind of personal failure as a child of God may run as deep and painful as it was for Judas or Peter when they had failed Christ. In the face of such humiliation, even the child of God needs to choose a pathway moving forward. For Judas, his failure led to death. For Peter, his choices led to life. If that realization of failing Christ came because of the conviction of the Spirit, there is always hope. In this context, hope comes in the framework of ask, seek, and knock.

THE POWER OF ASKING

The first reality of "asking" takes us right back to the request in Matthew 6:12 and the nature of our relationship with the heavenly Father. The reason Jesus did not define an object is because there are multiple relationships that may need to be addressed. While there is no defined sequence to these relationships that need healing and restoration, there may be a certain logic to the process.

Asking with Reference to their Heavenly Father

One of the important "asks" is to ask our heavenly Father to forgive us for having an unforgiving spirit. This relationship is the foundation for all other relationships. Only our heavenly Father can provide the perfect sense of love, mercy, grace, and forgiveness to properly restore His children to Himself. But this has always been the refuge to restore self-worth, significance, and security. Without this "ask," there is never hope to provide new life. But without the hope of forgiveness, there is no way to move forward.

Because our heavenly Father delights in us, as He delights in His Son, He always is eager to forgive us. When our failure meets His forgiveness, then healing can begin, even for hypocrites. This was Peter's experience after the devastation of his failure. Only our heavenly Father can restore His children to Himself. He alone can provide a place of healing and security to restore self-worth. This is not about forgiving ourselves as much as learning to embrace God's forgiveness.

ASKING WITH REFERENCE TO OTHER BELIEVERS

The second "ask" is to ask forgiveness from all the people we have judged, criticized, and complained about because of an unforgiving attitude, both in the family of God and even from unbelievers, with whom we dishonored the Lord with a bad attitude. If any of the disciples refused to forgive others, this automatically violated the character of their heavenly Father.

To borrow Paul's language, godly sorrow always produces repentance without regret, which leads to salvation, while worldly sorrow produces death (2 Corinthians 7:10-11). This is the key difference between Judas and Peter. Judas embraced worldly sorrow and it led to death. Peter experienced true godly sorrow that led to life. There is always a clear distinction and pathway between the two.

Asking in this context logically implies asking forgiveness for specific actions driven by an unforgiving heart. This will always be a painful and humiliating process. But, in following the example of our heavenly Father to always be ready to forgive, it will always lead to life. Forgiveness is always the doorway to healing. Deep healing follows forgiveness, not the other way around. But the promise is clear: whoever asks, receives. Under these circumstances and in this context, there is nothing more important than asking for forgiveness and God's guarantee of forgiveness.

SEEKING SECOND CHANCES

The second activity, "seeking," ought to be seen in light of the betrayal of throwing pearls before swine. With the Father's forgiveness lifting the weight of failure off our shoulders, the child of God now has the freedom and confidence to realign their heart with God's priorities, which has become completely out of alignment when their life was driven by a spirit of unforgiveness.

Anyone, once forgiven, can now freely *seek* first the kingdom of God and His righteousness. This may sound obvious, but many in God's family have simply walked away from their faith because of being hurt by the failures of others and, many times, because of their own failures. When forgiveness is not extended or truly experienced, then all desire to seek a new beginning with God, to re-engage His kingdom work, and live righteously, disappears.

KNOCKING FOR NEW OPPORTUNITIES

The idea of "knocking" is related to having a door opened (Matthew 7:8). This completes the recovery after the hypocrisy of unforgiveness. First, there is asking, specifically asking for forgiveness; second, there is seeking to realign one's life with God's kingdom purpose, His will, and righteousness. Finally, there is knocking, so that the Father will open new doors – doors of new opportunities that felt gone forever. Finding an open door is Christ's encouragement that the Father provides second chances and new opportunities. His kingdom work and doing His will has always involved flawed, broken people who will never do it perfectly. The Father has always used flawed human beings (outside of His Son).

The challenge for the disciples was to discover what new opportunities Jesus was discussing. To some extent, the collateral damage of unforgiveness would appear to close every door to serving the Lord or sharing the good news of the gospel. Behavior-driven by unforgiveness breaks trust and damages so many relationships that common sense would suggest there could never be open doors ever again. In spite of failure, our heavenly Father can open new doors for service, relationship, and ministry.

This was certainly true of Peter. In spite of denying Christ, Jesus forgave Peter. But when Jesus met with him on the shore, as described in John 21:15-17, Jesus did something quite extraordinary. When most people fail, they are convinced they will be shunned and ostracized. There is always the feeling of shame, and they fear they will never be welcomed back into the community. But Jesus did not come to Peter, urgently reassuring him of His love and encouragement. This is often the practice of many and with all good intentions. We want the person who failed to know we will help them no matter what. We reaffirm our love for them, our encouragement, and our acceptance. Jesus did not do that. His presence was all that He offered Peter.

What Jesus did was ask Peter if he loved Him. He didn't just do it once, but three times. He asked him three different ways. The point Jesus made is simple. The issue was never if Jesus loved Peter. Jesus, time and again, constantly demonstrated His love for His men. He taught them, lived with them, helped them, and involved them in His life. He now comes to Peter after the resurrection – which reminds us He also died for Peter - and asked if Peter truly loved Him. There was never any question about Jesus's posture.

After the third time Jesus asked Peter if he loved Him, Peter was grieved and frankly did not know what to say or do in response to Jesus's query. Jesus's response was to open the door for Peter to serve – "Feed my sheep." God's will, in His own time and purpose, opens up doors for His children to serve Him again, regardless of our personal failures. It may be in these kinds of circumstances that the child of God may discover the deepest levels of God's grace and mercy that they could never experience except in these scenarios. These open doors may take time, but our heavenly Father is the architect of new beginnings.

THE NATURE OF TRUE FORGIVENESS

Forgiveness does not mean there are no consequences to our choices. Doors that were open to some are often permanently closed. New opportunities may be completely different than what a person wanted or expected. Some would like to hold a person's failure over their head for a lifetime, which is not forgiveness at all. Others want their failures to disappear quickly out of sight in order to jump back into ministry. Healing and restoring trust follow forgiveness, but they do not replace it.

Forgiveness does not mean people will forget, either. Sometimes, there is a long pathway to rebuilding trust and a trustworthy reputation, but it can be done. Forgiveness releases a person from the guilt of their transgression, but that does not mean they are ready to jump back into things like nothing happened. It takes those around them a long time to rebuild trust because they do not want to be victims a second time. The greatest obstacle to restoring trust is often our own impatience to get back what we want.

There is always a cost to forgiveness. *A person must be willing to live with the consequences of another's actions because they believe God will stand in the gap between what they have lost and where they could have been if no offense had ever taken place.* The simple reality is that people's bad behavior causes others to be victims. There is always a cost to forgiveness because we can't always go back and change the past. We have to learn to move forward.

THE COST OF TRUE FORGIVENESS

When people owe a debt, sin against someone, or transgress the trust of a friend, there is always a sense of loss or betrayal. If someone owes a thousand dollars and they do not pay it back, the lender loses that money. If someone steals something from another and the victim is unable to get it back, they are the one who suffers the loss.

Forgiveness is often very costly because someone has to live with the consequences. Sometimes, that cost is emotional peace. Other times, people lose something more tangible, like money. Sometimes, sin costs us relationships, and our own credibility is damaged by the actions of another. We can lose opportunities because of someone's interference. When people betray us, they take something that we believe belongs to us. Everyone will struggle with loss because it always feels like the perpetrator, whether caught or not, is still getting away with something.

The problem for the disciples, like anyone, was that forgiveness does not always appear to resolve everything. Forgiving someone does not make all issues magically disappear. Forgiveness does not guarantee that this person won't turn around and do the same thing to someone else. Forgiveness is not romantic idealism where people forgive, all is restored, and everyone lives happily ever after.

In this narrative, Jesus points out the reality that forgiving someone comes with a cost, and doing so requires a new commitment to trusting our heavenly Father in new ways.

The willingness to forgive says much more about what we believe God will do for us than what people have done to us. If we do not believe God will properly deal with the injustice that we have experienced, it is impossible to forgive. We instinctively want to know that they won't get away with hurting us or others. If we don't believe God will handle this properly, we will continue to cling to our hurt and find ways to execute our own form of justice. The critical component to forgiveness is believing that our heavenly Father has our back and is willing to stand with us, providing what we need:

"Or what man is there among you, when his son shall ask him for a loaf, will give him a stone? Or if he shall ask for a fish, he will not give him a snake, will he? If then you being evil, know how to give good gifts to your children, how much more shall your Father who is in heaven give what is good to those who ask Him!"

Matthew 7:9-11, NASB1977

GOD'S PROMISE TO PROVIDE

Jesus continues the theme of "asking," but it shifts from the context of being restored from the hypocrisy of unforgiveness to providing for His children when they choose to forgive. He maintains the continuity of focus by using the example that if earthly fathers, who are evil, desire to give good gifts to their children, how much more will our heavenly Father give to those who ask Him. The principle truth is subtle, but there are clues in the text to help us see the nature of the Father's goodness towards His children.

Of course, many would argue that this whole section has nothing to do with the hypocrisy of the first six verses. The tenor of these texts was simply to remind the disciples that the Father will provide for their needs. But Jesus framed His teaching around some important considerations. First, the context of warning about hypocrisy does require a response, and Jesus provides the solution in verses seven and eight. It would be uncharacteristic of Jesus to have warned his men about these dangers and not explain a redemptive component to the worst-case scenario explained in the first six verses.

Secondly, Jesus had already taught His men how to ask God for daily provisions through the request, "Give us this day our daily bread." Simply repeating that again without a distinct difference becomes redundant. It stands to reason that the context has changed from providing for everyday needs to a more severe situation dealing with significant loss based on the extreme hypocrisy of others.

Thirdly, the nature of restoration from unforgiveness, moving forward with the heavenly Father, is both necessary and relevant to the narrative and the context. His disciples needed guidance on what to expect from God when they chose to forgive. Jesus taught that our heavenly Father has our back no matter our need, or, in this case, crisis. If God's children suffer any loss by forgiving anyone that leaves them vulnerable, Jesus taught their Father will provide for them. Jesus verified His point by referring back to His temptation experience, showing how much the Father cares about us even in the face of great sacrifice. Jesus presents two propositions:

The first scenario is that if one asks for bread, a father will not give him a stone. This was the exact circumstance of Jesus's temptation in reverse. Jesus was tempted by the devil to turn stones into bread since He had fasted for forty days. The devil sought to convince Jesus to place His own needs above the Father's will, to take matters into His own hands. When Jesus was most vulnerable, He chose to trust the will of the Father over taking matters into His own hands.

When a child of God has been hurt by someone he needs to forgive, the temptation is to take matters into their own hands. When a child of God makes the personal commitment to forgive others, especially in the face of personal loss, Jesus promises that our heavenly Father will provide for them in spite of their sacrifice. The Father is sufficient to stand in the gap and provide for His children. This guiding principle Jesus taught in Matthew 7:9-11 is best captured by an Old Testament character named Joseph when he revealed himself to his brothers for the first time:

"But Joseph said to them, "Do not fear, for am I in the place of God? As for you, you meant evil against me, but God meant it for good, to bring it about that many people should be kept alive, as they are today."

Genesis 50:19-20

Joseph had every reason to resent his brothers for the evil they did in selling him to traders. This betrayal cost him the life he could have had at home. Everything he knew was stripped away because of the vindictiveness of his brothers. When they finally came face to face, he had the power to get even, but he chose to provide and care for them instead (Genesis 50:19-21). He believed that God was with him and used even these terrible circumstances to get him exactly where God desired.

Jesus taught His disciples the same basic principle. Their heavenly Father would care and provide for them even if others had done things that changed the very trajectory of their life. Even when people intend to do evil things to God's children, God will take even the most difficult challenges and use them for good. His children need to learn to trust Him so that regardless of whatever suffering we experience, He will be with them and care for them. We must have confidence that God will guide us through trials for our ultimate good. The challenge, however, is that if we are not convinced that God's "alternative journey" is for our good, we are more than likely to be angry with God because He did not fulfill our plans.

Jesus was careful not to promise that God will replace or restore what we have lost. He will provide for what we need. Through our loss, we learn to trust Him and His will. We are now in a different place, on a new trajectory, but exactly where God wants us to be for His purpose and glory.

LOOKING AFTER OUR NEEDS

The second statement is about asking for a fish and not receiving a snake. While this reference is far more indirect, it would be common for snakes to inhabit the wilderness where Jesus was tempted. Again this focused on providing for basic provision in life, not necessarily the desires of life. Jesus's final statement is intended to reinforce the same principle. If our earthly fathers who are evil can give good gifts, how much more will our heavenly Father give to those who ask Him? We need to implicitly trust Him regardless of what others do to us. God will always be for us:

> "So whatever you wish that others would do to you, do also to them, for this is the Law and the Prophets."
>
> Matthew 7:12

The final words of Jesus are powerful when it comes to understanding the whole picture of unforgiveness and the power of forgiveness. His final summary of His entire teaching is the underlying principle to carry the disciples through the difficult issue of relationships.

The "golden rule," as many label it, is often extracted from this text as an isolated principle. Fortunately, this is one of the few principles that has the capacity to be applied to almost any relationship and circumstance. But there is value in considering how this verse connects to the context.

This simple admonition is the perfect capstone to Jesus's teaching on forgiveness. The dangers of unforgiveness and the command to forgive others may seem inevitable in a broken and sinful world, but Jesus is guiding us to consider how we treat those around us.

Anyone who does not want to be hurt by others ought to demonstrate care when communicating with others. Everyone who has been hurt by someone knows the pain, struggle, and hurt that comes from conflict. The simple truth is that if I treat others the way I want to be treated, a great deal of pain, suffering, and conflict can be avoided. That being said, it is even more critical to understand this truth in the conflict of human relationships.

While this axiom applies to life in general, it is particularly pertinent to remember that the disciples were instructed to pray, "Forgive us our debts as we forgive our debtors." Clearly, even in the most painful experiences where people can take advantage of others, from manipulation to moral evil, our heavenly Father expects His children to value everyone, treat them with respect, and forgive as He has forgiven.

In the larger context of Jesus's sermon on the Mount, Jesus already drew attention to this truth: Love your enemies and pray for those who persecute you. If His followers only love those who love them, there is no reward. The best way to act is the way our Father acts.

PRINCIPLES ON THE COST OF FORGIVENESS:

1. Forgiveness is costly but necessary to remain spiritually healthy and honor our heavenly Father.

   - How challenging has it been for you to forgive others when you have been hurt by them?
   - Are you aware of people who have been "angry" their whole life towards family or friends because they have been hurt by them?

2. Only those who actually believe their heavenly Father has their back and will ultimately deal justly with sin and know how to forgive others.

   - How convinced are you that God has your back?
   - What are you willing to entrust to your Heavenly Father and "let go"?

3. No matter how significant our hypocrisy, personal failure, or moral indiscretion, God always provides a pathway to find forgiveness, restoration, and new opportunities to connect with Him and serve His purpose.

   - Do you have moral failures that you feel are unrecoverable?
   - How do the truths from the Lord's Prayer provide hope in the midst of failure?

4. Our willingness to forgive others says more about what we believe God can do for us above what people have done to us.

   - Do you believe in this principle for your own life? Why or why not?
   - What would this truth look like in your life if you truly embraced it?

PRAYER

Heavenly Father, help me to value your forgiveness in my life, both in my salvation and my ongoing walk with you. May I understand your grace to forgive others even when I feel deeply hurt by their actions toward me. Help me understand the serious nature of harboring unforgiveness and how damaging it can be to myself, to others, and to my relationship with you. Amen.

CHAPTER 7

PICK A LANE

Choosing the Right Path
for Your Life

"And lead us not into temptation…"

Matthew 6:13

"Enter by the narrow gate. For the gate is wide, and the way is broad that leads to destruction, and many are those who enter by it. For the gate is small, and the way is narrow that leads to life, and there are few who find it."

Matthew 7:13-23, NASB1977

Before I agree to perform a wedding ceremony, I require the couple to go through premarital counseling—regardless of whether I meet with them or if they connect with another counselor. Counseling provides an assessment of their relationship and a process to address needs, improve relational skills, and prepare them for their marriage journey.

When Barb and I were going through premarital counseling, our pastor (who happened to be Barb's uncle) shared one critical truth with us that I have never forgotten: our ability to deal with conflict and resolve our differences would ultimately determine if our marriage would last. The purpose of counseling was to give us the skills to prepare for such challenges.

All that sounds good until you are actually married, trying to work out life in the same space. We married, went on our honeymoon, and immediately stepped into my first pastorate in a little village church in central Alberta. The first year was rough for both of us as we struggled to figure out how to adjust to marriage and ministry. Premarital counseling gave us the right information, but it was quite another thing to put all that into practice in the context of real life. We were on a whole new learning curve in the context of real-life marriage.

DOES GOD TEMPT US?

No other statement in the Lord's Prayer creates more tension than when Jesus taught the disciples to ask the Father to not lead them into temptation. To suggest that God would lead anyone into temptation sounds inappropriate and almost blasphemous. Acknowledging that the Greek term can be translated as both "temptation" and "trials" does not always ease the anxiety. The vast majority of scholars translate this term as temptation, even though some have suggested this could also mean trials or extreme testing.

For the disciples to ask their Father to not lead them into temptation suggests that He might actually do such a thing. Most assume He would never lead anyone into temptation because it violates His very character. He who is holy cannot do what is evil. James 1:13-16 clearly states, "God cannot be tempted by evil and He Himself does not tempt anyone." Somehow, this request in the Lord's Prayer and the truth claim in the book of James need to be reconciled.

However, the wilderness text is very clear. The Spirit led or compelled Jesus into the wilderness to be tempted by the devil. This was not a matter of God simply permitting this to happen. Instead, there was a clear intention to place Jesus in a context where He was to be tempted by the devil.

This event cannot be relegated to general trials (James 1:2-3). The obvious reason Jesus taught His men to ask the Father to not lead them into temptation was because this was His exact experience in the wilderness. Consequently, to understand the value of this portion of the prayer requires some clarity. Passively acknowledging this request in prayer is profoundly different than understanding the critical significance of avoiding the spiritual landmines.

The question was never whether they would face severe testing but when. The question was not whether God would lead them directly into a faceoff with the devil or if He was simply permitting it. This was the very nature of living for Christ in a world damaged by evil. Therefore, we will also face trials and temptations (John 16:33).

We need to know with unshakable confidence that our heavenly Father has His fingerprints on every aspect of our journey and is always present. If our Father is present, then He has a purpose for every experience, even in the face of extreme tests and temptations. No matter what circumstances we face, His desire is *always* to strengthen our faith and affirm godly character, never to see us fail.

The obvious challenge is how to think about God leading His children into temptation. This is a hard concept for anyone because it feels wrong. Sometimes, we must work through complexity in order to get to simplicity; we need to fight through confusion to get to clarity.

In the context of the Lord's Prayer, the point of this request is asking the Father not to lead His children into a context of extreme testing in which God gives the devil permission to be part of that test. God's desire is to demonstrate the character of His children and cultivate faith. Satan's desire is to turn the upright from their relationship with the Father.

THE TEMPTATION OF JOB

Outside of Christ's temptation, the perfect example of this is Job. We know God gave permission to Satan to have the power to test Job. We know it was a test because God held him up as His servant who was blameless and upright, fearing God and turning away from evil. Satan mocked God and accused Him of over-protecting Job; Satan claimed that Job was only upright because God had made his life easy and sheltered from hardship and suffering. Satan posited that if Job experienced severe hardships, he would "curse God to His face." (Job 1:10-11).

While God did nothing other than give Satan permission to test Job, He defined the limits of what Satan was permitted to do. God cannot be tempted by evil, and He Himself does not personally tempt anyone to sin or evil. Although He allowed the evil one to inflict a litany of extreme afflictions upon Job, God's purpose was always to demonstrate the uprightness of his life. God never personally tempted Job, and using Satan as an intermediary agent does not implicate God to have evil motives. This may seem to be unacceptable semantics to some, but in reality it is an important nuance. God's purpose is always to validate the character and faith of His people.

Satan's desire was to destroy Job's faith. Even though Job was ignorant of the conversation behind an eternal veil and unaware of Satan's personal involvement, Job did not sin, nor did he blame

God. Satan's affliction on Job included some horrible actions towards his family and possessions with the intent to tempt him to question God's goodness and reject Him. Job had no idea that Satan was the catalyst to all the suffering.

In the same way, we are often ignorant of God's ways, but we should never question His care for us. Satan's activity in the world is to inflict evil and suffering on everyone in order to blind the eyes of the unbelieving and tempt God's people to do evil by rejecting our heavenly Father. When we are tempted to blame God for doing evil, we ignore the truth. He cannot be tempted by evil, and He does not tempt anyone to do evil. But we also cannot ignore the reality that there is a spiritual conflict that engulfs this broken world and often drags us into experiences of suffering, hardship, and even temptations.

FACING TEMPTATIONS

The first temptation Jesus exposed to His disciples contrasted a narrow gate and pathway with a wide gate and wide pathway. The purpose was to train and equip them to overcome evil and serve in His kingdom. The narrow gate inaugurated the journey on the narrow pathway. A familial relationship with God is the gateway to living out the responsibilities the Father expected from that relationship. Relationships always precede responsibilities. Jesus came preaching the gospel of the kingdom, inviting Israel back into fellowship with the God of their forefathers, which was the doorway to restoring the coming kingdom.

The narrow pathway, outlined in chapters 6:14 through 7:27, with all of its eternal values and divine priorities defined the nature and substance of this path. One could make the argument that the Sermon on the Mount, in its entirety, starting in Matthew 5:2, embodies this narrow path; it is His divine blueprint for His people to live godly in a broken world. It is also the pathway that rises above the Law to reflect the true character of God through His people. This is anything but easy, and it demands divine resources and a godly perspective. This helps develop spiritual resilience to truly follow Jesus on this path. This pathway would never be attractive to an unbeliever, and it will always be challenging for even the sincerest disciple. The prayer is a stern warning that the narrow pathway is laden with spiritual landmines and relational pitfalls that can undermine that journey.

On the one hand, there is a simple distinction between the narrow path and the broad way. Clearly, the narrow way embraces the way God has called His people to live, and the broad way is not approved by the Father. In the narrative that follows, Jesus explains that those who walk the broad way include the false prophets and those who think they have done great things for Christ, but both end up being rejected. On this basis, the primary comparison is between those who are believers and those who are not.

Those who walk the narrow path will cross paths with those on the wide pathway. But this will be more than just crossing paths; Jesus knew they would inevitably collide with those on the wide path. He has warned of these dangers, but we need to be trained to respond God's way. It is the only way to deal with temptation and evil.

But the practical reality of these two pathways is not quite so clear. Jesus set this prayer and His commentary in the cultural context of the hypocrisy of the religion of the times. The pure and undefiled teaching of Jesus called Israel to repent and believe in the gospel. Their hypocrisy was the result of an unhealthy people of God who had lost their way. They had moved off the narrow pathway to walk the broad way, but this did not seal their fate. Jesus offered a second chance to the hypocrites through repentance and believing in the gospel.

THE NATURE OF THE NARROW PATH

Jesus warned His disciples of a number of spiritual landmines and relational pitfalls. These obstacles could hinder their ability to walk the narrow path. These dangers had the potential to push the disciples from the narrow path to stride on the wide pathway, which was easier and far more popular. This idea of a pathway indicates a journey; the way we live is dictated by our own choices. As indicated previously, the concern is about the way we choose to live, not a lifestyle.

The nature of having a relationship with a holy God in a world damaged by evil always forces spiritual choices that keep us in fellowship with our heavenly Father or push us onto another pathway. In such circumstances, due to His love for us, our Father diligently pursues His children to give us a chance to step back onto the narrow pathway. The presence of Jesus is a testament to the Father's love for His people.

When His disciples live on the narrow way, they thrive on the power of their relationship with their heavenly Father. The most life-giving reality from Him is His forgiveness. A holy God requires a posture of humility. Our identity as children of God provides the ultimate clarity of self-worth. Our sense of significance is defined by our Father's purpose, and security is wrapped around the unchanging nature of Jesus, not the vacillating chaos of the world.

People on this narrow path treasure up things in heaven and not on earth. They keep their eyes fixed on eternal things, and it is evident they have only one Master they serve. The narrow way provides a deep rest for the soul because of reliance upon the Father. This, in turn, provides the freedom to eagerly seek after His kingdom and righteousness.

People on the narrow way will experience the inexhaustible power of forgiveness in their own lives, which empowers them to forgive others. They have learned how destructive unforgiveness impacts themselves, others, and their relationship with God. They will not allow the truth of treating others the way they would want others to treat them to ever become a cliche. Those who live on this narrow pathway will have great conviction of the power of His personal presence. They know that regardless of how they have been treated by others, they are never alone because God is with them. This is the power of the narrow gate and narrow way.

Asking the Father to not lead us into temptation is a request not unlike Jesus's plea in the Garden of Gethsemane. He pleaded earnestly in the face of extreme testing and temptation that the Father would explore another pathway. Yet Jesus deferred to the Father's will, not His own. He faced the dilemma that His Father's will, the narrow path that led straight to a crucible of suffering, would take every ounce of spiritual focus and conviction He had taught in His prayer. He chose to follow the Father's leading through this excruciating journey of suffering for the sake of the Father's redemptive purpose.

This was not a new dilemma. Jesus's temptations in the wilderness was the narrow pathway upon which the Spirit led Jesus, where the Father allowed His Son to go through a litany of severe temptations at the hand of the devil. The devil's tactic was simple: if you are the Son of God, prove it. All three attempts were aimed at compromising the Son's relationship with the Father, which was non-negotiable from Jesus's perspective. Jesus never deviated from that pathway.

LIVE AND LEARN

In the same way, Jesus trained His disciples to have the spiritual strength to endure temptations and have the confidence to trust the Father through those tests. This narrow pathway needs divine focus and empowerment. Otherwise, the constant temptation to follow a less demanding pathway that was easier to walk with lots of company is compelling.

Most people live and learn. Everyone makes mistakes and regrets poor choices. No one makes perfect decisions all the time, and the reality is that most would change many decisions they made. We learn from our failures and make adjustments. Most realize the damage of their decisions, so they do not make the same mistakes.

Everyone gains wisdom about the subtle temptations that lured them into choices that looked great at the time but resulted in much hardship and loss. Many also learn by paying attention to the mistakes and failures of others, not with a cynical or condemning attitude but with deep compassion. They take note of what may have snagged a fellow believer and, with much humility, heed the warning signs of temptation that can so easily entangle the sincerest follower of Jesus.

The sad component of our experiences is that we often live without learning. We make mistakes like everyone, but we think that we will never be caught off guard again. People deceive themselves when they think they are wiser and smarter, so they begin to rely on their own common sense to figure out what God wants rather than simply submitting to His wisdom, not just in difficult situations but for all of life.

There are some who keep making the same mistakes over and over, stumbling into temptations that briefly fill some vacancy in their soul but soon vaporize into memory. The collateral damage often leaves their hearts more broken and despondent than before. Fewer things weigh heavier on the soul than the repetitive failure to overcome personal sin. Those deep, internal struggles deprive an individual of the grace and forgiveness extended by our heavenly Father. One of the key reasons individuals eventually leave the church is when they lose hope to genuinely experience the power of God to transform the damage in their own heart.

The Lord's Prayer was designed to teach His disciples to learn and live. Divine wisdom directly communicates the heart of the Father, through His Son, to His children. It contains no voluminous outlines nor extensive details for every aspect of life. This is the most concise and clearest communication of the Father to His children so that we may know how to live in a broken world. This is the foundation, the bedrock non-negotiables, that God promises will help His children avoid the poisonous temptations of the heart and protect us from becoming hard-hearted over the failures of others and ourselves.

But unless His children know how to make right choices in the crucible of severe testing or temptation, it takes only one weak moment to destroy faith and cultivate a bitter spirit. We must learn so we may live and live well. But the temptations are subtle and dangerous. Since the broadway is where the majority travel, bated by peer pressure, it provides a dangerous temptation that is hard to resist.

This broad way is like a blurry silhouette of the narrow way. It is a defective replica of the narrow gate and pathway. The gate is wide, and the way is broad, which leads to destruction. Both the narrow way and the broad way are not physical pathways; they are pathways of the heart. Every individual who goes through this gate and walks the broad path may also be convinced that they have a relationship with the Father and are doing what the Father desires.

Since the broad way can look similar to the narrow way but diverge enough to not actually be the narrow way, it is by necessity a departure so subtle that it camouflages its true nature to be convinced otherwise. It neglects relationship with the Father and deviates from the responsibilities of kingdom life, yet leaves the individual convinced that they are in good standing with God.

The religion of the Pharisees and scribes is a perfect portrait of individuals who were absolutely convinced they were on the narrow path but found themselves walking the broad way. It had become a systemic problem that had no hope of repair. Jesus did not call Israel to add God to their system; He called them to abandon a system that was the broad way. Israel, as a whole, was not treating God as holy. They were not doing His will. Their motivation for community was strictly grounded in rules, regulations, and religion. Israel had lost their way. Christ's announcement of His coming kingdom and the proclamation of the gospel was a call to return to the narrow pathway.

THE DANGER OF THE WIDE PATH

One of the challenges of American Christianity has been the temptation to be lured onto the wide pathway over the narrow pathway of relationship with the Father and commitment to kingdom priorities. There are many wide gates that can push the church to the wide path, and even things with good intentions can become the wider pathway.

Churches have constantly sought to be relevant to the culture. This may seem perfectly appropriate until being relevant becomes more important than the gospel. Many have ignored that the end does not justify the means. The concern to ignite mission in the heart of believers has often started with the wrong question: how to be relevant to the culture. This then creates pathways to train believers to be relevant rather than righteous.

THE WIDE PATH

The gospel is relevant to broken humans and our common struggles with sin and evil. It provides the context by which hope shines like a radiant light in the darkness. It is the foolishness of the gospel that is the power of God, not the relevance of human wisdom, that changes hearts and provides hope. We have relied more on our skill than our Savior.

An obsession with managing programs has subtly replaced growing people. Personal preference often starts with holy convictions but ends up becoming the litmus test for spiritual maturity. The temptation to worship the style of music over worshiping the One behind the music has crippled and even divided churches. It is apparent that the gospel is not the centerpiece of some people or even churches. The struggle for doing something relevant has turned the gospel into a marketing project. There is always the temptation to step away from Paul's declaration: "My message and my preaching were not in persuasive words of wisdom, but in demonstration of the Spirit and power that your faith should not rest on the wisdom of men, but on the power of God" (1 Corinthians 2:4-5, NASB1977).

Leaving a legacy often results in building our own kingdom rather than serving His kingdom. The subtle temptation is that any of these things can start with the best of intentions but often become the doorway to wide and popular pathways that undermine our relationship with Christ and exchange His kingdom work for our own.

Denominationalism has unwittingly contributed to this wide pathway, and it is likely that most of us have journeyed here at some point. Denominations have created their own culture, infrastructure, traditions, and practices. Most are built on unique distinctions based on Biblical truth, principles, ideas, or convictions. While all these things can have legitimacy, they can also push individuals a few degrees off the narrow path to create a broader pathway that everyone loves, often because it feels relevant but not spiritually helpful. The forms of religion become more important than the transformation of the heart. If you asked the Pharisees and the scribes, they thought they had it all figured out too. This was precisely what Paul was concerned about in the book of Colossians:

> "If with Christ you died to the elemental spirits of the world, why, as if you were still alive in the world, do you submit to regulations— "Do not handle, Do not taste, Do not touch" (referring to things that all perish as they are used)—according to human precepts and teachings? These have indeed an appearance of wisdom in promoting self-made religion and asceticism and severity to the body, but they are of no value in stopping the indulgence of the flesh –"
>
> Colossians 2:20-23

Creating a broad pathway is nothing new. Most would think that the broad way is simply the way of the devil, and in some respects, it is. He is certainly a proponent of undermining any relationship with the Father, and he is fully committed to destroying His kingdom work. But often, the distinction between the narrow way and the broad path is much more fluid than what we may think.

Churches will always create pathways to help believers grow. The struggle is creating pathways that effectively bring life-change. Some leaders have even raised concerns over the effectiveness of small groups. They can become insulated huddles for nothing better than ingrown fellowship groups. Everyone desires the narrow path, but it is far too easy to create a wide pathway.

People have readily been compliant to participate with many programs and structures offered by churches, but many have found them to be empty. One can argue that life change is the responsibility of the person, not the program, which, if true, would raise the question of why churches have relied so heavily on programs over the years. But compliance does not mean commitment. The greatest temptations for churches is an endless amount of structures, programs, rules, regulations, and traditions to be a growing, effective church, but we may have inadvertently created a wide pathway that does not produce life in and of itself.

Many people have had teachable hearts and prospered from being involved in church structures and ministries. We can find many people whose lives have been profoundly changed by others investing in them in a faith community. That being said, the worst-case scenario would be people holding to a form of godliness while denying its power (2 Timothy 3:5). Managing programs rather than investing in people has placed many on a broad pathway. The current mode of many deconstructing their faith and walking away from the church is clear evidence that our best intentions have often fallen short of meaningful change.

Instead of celebrating our unity in Christ, we obsess over distinctions that often divide the greater body of Christ and create unique pathways to serving God and His kingdom work. For some, it is the gospel, while others focus on social justice issues and ethnic conflict. Others advocate the aspect of love and acceptance in an increasingly divided world.

Every church has its doorways and pathways they believe create spiritual maturity and disciples. Every church would claim to have an answer to the relationship with the Father and the nature of true kingdom responsibility. All these are legitimate convictions. But if these are not grounded as an outworking of being on the narrow pathway, they can become a wider gate that leads down a broad pathway.

On the other hand, there are many churches that have a serious mess on their hands. They have not grasped that having no plan or pathway for believers can be as damaging as having a legalistic, performance-driven process that keeps people from the kingdom. These churches are usually shaped by personal preference, leaving the church stagnant and unhealthy. This exacerbates the wide path and hinders people from having a genuine relationship with the Father.

THE WIDE PATH OF IDEOLOGY

The other contribution to the broad way is ideology. Ideology often conflicts with our theology. Both ideology and theology are different types of worldviews. Neither are inherently right or wrong in and of themselves, but they may have a hard time co-existing.

Ideology is a worldview firmly anchored in first-world concerns. Conflicts about our world and culture are the exposed nerve of living in a world damaged by evil and sin. One can make an endless list of possible candidates to rally around: everything from global warming to social justice, ethnic discrimination, inequality, Christian nationalism, politics, and economic instability – these are real problems that need attention.

We often think that people who are in our churches are going down a narrow pathway to become disciples of Christ. The reality is that they have been on a broader pathway for their particular cause. While theology was part of their life, it is not what drives their life.

Believers ought to have concern for these things, but many have stepped away from the central message of the gospel to make their cause the centerpiece of their life or church. There is a difference between Christ's mission for us in the world and our contextual vision to impact our community. If these are reversed so that the local or cultural cause takes over the mission of Christ, then the church may become relevant at the risk of being spiritually ineffective.

It might help to illustrate the conflict of interest. If a person loves animals and describes themselves as an animal lover, he or she might support the SPCA (Society for the Prevention of Cruelty to Animals), own a pet and even become a foster parent for abused animals. The person is passionate about animals. He or she knows the various breeds, care techniques, feeding requirements, and unique training procedures for different animals. This would qualify as an ideology – this is what drives and motivates his or her life. It is not wrong unless it begins to take precedence over theology.

If this animal lover was transported back to the time of Old Testament Israel under the sacrificial system, it wouldn't be surprising if he or she was mortified by the practice of animal sacrifices. They would see those practices as horrid, brutal, and abusive towards animals and might try to have it stopped.

This person might urgently appeal to the priests to stop this brutality to animals. We can almost imagine them starting demonstrations to change the system and dismantle these archaic practices. His or her final appeal might be to the High Priest as the final authority to bring this system to a stop. The High Priest would, in turn, explain that this was what God commanded His people to do to have a relationship with Him. The animal lover might, in their frustration, blurt out, "Then your God must be wrong! You can't do these things to these animals!"

While I love animals and had some pets growing up, this passion may cause some conflict with theology. This obviously is an extreme example and not particularly relevant now, but it has been this kind of ideology that has been tearing away at the church for years. Ideology can be at odds with theology in so many ways, but it does not have to be.

Theology is the perspective and worldview of the eternal, created by brilliant but finite minds to help us grasp the unfamiliar and define our finite reality in relationship to our Creator. But theological systems are not infallible, and they are certainly not equal to the inerrant revelation of the Scriptures. Theological debate can be extremely helpful to explore the infinite, and those who travel the narrow pathway are stimulated by learning from others. However, the danger is when people hold to their theological convictions more tightly than the Scriptures themselves.

Those on the broad path often weaponize their theology to judge and condemn others who do not agree with them. They treat their theology as equal to God's Word, and maybe it does not surprise us that this mindset has created strong divisions among different groups of Christian denominations. Clearly, the legalistic theology of the Pharisees and Scribes conflicted with the teachings of Jesus. The issue is not that we have much to learn from one another. The danger is when our thoughts about God replace the revelation from God.

Certain essential doctrines define the nature of Christianity, which are not negotiable, but we have mastered the ability to micromanage truth and find new and creative ways to divide rather than find common ground toward unity.

I had a pastor share a story with me about a church gathering where one of his members accused him of being a Calvinist because he was preaching from the first chapter of Ephesians; apparently, Ephesians is a Calvinistic book and should not be preached in that particular church. Even if we disagree, there is a need for respect and grace that humbly searches for truth, not condemnation!

Both ideology and theology have limits, and there have been some stringent wars over Biblical issues too. To borrow the language of the Lord's commentary, many churches have shifted to walk the wide path. We do not have an "open hand" policy to keep on listening and learning from one another for the purpose of discovering a greater love for Christ and an increasing faith in our heavenly Father.

We like to be right, and we often weaponize our convictions to judge others. No matter how much education you have, no matter how long you have been a Christian, how many verses you have memorized, how many leadership teams you have been on, no matter how smart we think we are, in the eyes of our heavenly Father, we are a bunch of four-year-olds, strutting around with our chest puffed out, and too often fighting over each other's toys.

The narrow pathway cannot be measured by church practices or traditions. This does not mean that these are not meaningful, as varied and different as they may be between different church movements. All these practices will always be an occasion to deepen faith but not a guarantee of faith. I don't see anything we do in our church, child dedication, baptism, communion, membership, or holding any positions of leadership, as the guarantee of faith but, at best, the expression of faithfulness, not to the program but to the Lord.

WHAT ARE THE ESSENTIALS?

Do people need to belong to our denomination to be right with God? Of course not! What every person needs is to believe in the character of God and have faith in His promises in Christ. When Jesus outlined the Lord's Prayer, the only practice we might extract from Jesus's teaching is prayer and fasting.

Jesus's model was investing in His men and not creating too many structures. The Lord's Prayer has none of the things that our modern-day church world holds dear. At the heart of everything is a relationship with our heavenly Father and a commitment to His kingdom and His righteousness.

I know all kinds of people who grew up in all kinds of church or denominational backgrounds, who went through baptisms, confirmations, Sunday School classes, communion service, and a membership process. They conformed to all the traditions and expectations of a faith community and then walked away from the church, now showing little to no interest in any meaningful relationship with Christ. There is always a danger of creating systems that have the appearance of wisdom in self-made religion but have no value against fleshly indulgences (Colossians 2:23).

SUBTLE SEGUES

Jesus taught about a narrow way and a broad way. Some may assume these pathways simply describe the path of followers of Christ compared to the journey of unbelievers. But the nature of Jesus's warnings implies that believers are not insulated from sliding into the broad path if they fail to live according to the spiritual blueprint of the prayer.

This is not confined to first-century Israel. The problem of finding ourselves on the broad way is just as real a temptation today as it was back then. Inevitably, there will be a huge mix of people on the broad way, and even God's children are susceptible to wandering off the narrow path and end up on the broad way. Since the narrow gate and narrow path was created by God, we can safely establish that the wide gate and wide path are not His design. Anything deviating from His pathway becomes the broad way that leads to all kinds of destruction.

Our heavenly Father may expose us or lead us into experiences that involve testing and even facing temptation so we can learn obedience from what we suffer. Faith is perfected under trials, and character is forged in the crucible of enduring temptations. Our Father always intends to see us grow our faith and our character. It is never a guarantee but an opportunity. The most subtle deception is getting caught on a pathway that actually hinders relationship with the Lord and diverts individuals off the essential responsibilities of the narrow pathway.

One expression of the broad gate and wide path essentially aligns with the religion of the Pharisees and scribes. Their hypocrisy was impressing people and demanding compliance to traditions and regulations that hinder people from the kingdom of God, all while being convinced they were the spiritual experts of relationship with the God of Israel. To suggest that we don't have the potential to do the same thing is short-sighted.

The only viable pathway is the one our heavenly Father created. Jesus taught this in the Lord's Prayer, which sets our relationship with Him as the first priority and His kingdom and will as our reality. Certainly, the rest of the Scriptures flesh out the details of such a Biblical blueprint for the way we should live. This is the foundation and the anchor to a God-honoring life. In order to be successful, we must learn to avoid the spiritual pitfalls that can cripple progress, resulting in an unfruitful life. The first test is to make sure we are always walking on the right path – His path.

PRINCIPLES ON WAKING THE NARROW PATH:

1. The gates and pathways are pathways of the heart, not physical pathways.

   • How do you decide what pathway you are walking presently?

   • How much are outward things a distraction to inner change?

2. The narrow gate means stepping into a relationship with the Father. The substance of the narrow pathway is defined by the Lord's Prayer and how Jesus interprets each section.

   • How familiar are you now with this narrow pathway given by Jesus?

   • How much has the Lord's Prayer influenced the way you live for the Lord? Why or why not?

3. A disciple who is known by the Father will find a Spirit-filled, God-honoring life walking the narrow pathway of seeking His kingdom and righteousness.

   • How complicated have you made your walk with Jesus currently?

   • What kinds of "religious things" have discouraged you in your walk with Christ?

4. The Lord's Prayer will help believers navigate the spiritual landmines and relational pitfalls that everyone faces as they walk the narrow pathway.

   • What truths from Jesus' commentary are exciting for you as you think about your relationship with your heavenly Father? Explain.

   • What excites you about re-engaging Jesus in your life?

5. A believer can become distracted and tempted to move to the wide pathway.

- What things are you struggling with that seem to be a constant struggle?
- What ways have you tried to overcome these obstacles? Why do you think you have been unsuccessful in overcoming these struggles?

PRAYER

Father, our greatest desire as those shepherding your flock is to have them love you with all their heart, all their soul, and all their strength. Help us, above all else, to shepherd their hearts so they are motivated by your grace, not by any compliance to earthly traditions. Protect us from creating a pathway that keeps their heart from loving you. Help me to take full responsibility for my walk with you. Teach my heart that I am responsible for my spiritual walk and my love for you. You have provided a faith community to encourage, support, and provide for me to shape my life according to my relationship with you as defined by Christ. The structures, programs, and ministries that are part of a faith community are designed to help me take the next steps of faith so that my life honors and glorifies you. While the place of community is special, the people are wonderful and inspiring. The programs are meaningful. Help my motivation be to Christ and His mission through your church for your honor and glory. Amen.

CHAPTER 8

THE TRAPS OF TEMPTATION

*How to Spot Traps and
Stay on Track*

"Beware of the false prophets, who come to you in sheep's clothing but inwardly are ravenous wolves. You will recognize them by their fruits. Are grapes gathered from thorn bushes, or figs from thistles? So, every healthy tree bears good fruit, but the bad tree bears bad fruit. A good tree cannot produce bad fruit, nor can a bad tree produce good fruit. Every tree that does not bear good fruit is cut down and thrown into the fire. Thus you will recognize them by their fruits."

Matthew 7:15-20

I have done my fair share of marriage counseling. Marriages that are highly contentious always feel one comment away from divorce. Counseling almost always begins with one partner who pours out their frustrations about problems in their relationship with their spouse. The story is heartbreaking and believable, so convincing at times that I have found myself frustrated at their spouse for creating such hardship!

However, when I finally get the chance to sit down with their spouse, I get the other side of the story. I find out there are some facts missing, I get a clearer understanding of the larger context, and we begin to dive into the complexity of motives and intentions. There is always overlap with the facts, but the real problem is how each person interprets those facts. The most challenging aspect of counseling is sorting out how two people who are supposed to love one another can become so conflicted over issues that seem inconsequential. The goal is not only to discover what is true but to restore trust.

One of the most challenging temptations or tests the disciples faced were false prophets. The essential nature of a false prophet means a person claims to speak for God, but their message is false; they do not truly represent the heart of God nor the Word of God. The nature of falsehood, or untruth, manifests itself in a multitude of ways. Truth can be miscommunicated by distorting the truth or simply communicating false information. The fact that Jesus refers to false prophets implies that individuals falsely represented Israel's God.

As a pastor, I have spent decades learning how critical it is to represent God's Word accurately. I have gleaned from the wisdom of professors and books explaining the seriousness of interpreting and preaching God's Word correctly. I have been taught philosophy related to interpreting Scriptures, which is intended to protect me from reading my own ideas back into the passage.

Understanding principles like context, culture, the definition of terms, the nature of different genres in the Scriptures, guidelines for extracting principles for our own context, and the role of analogy for present day application have all been imprinted on those who venture to teach from the holy Scriptures. All of this is to keep us from imposing our own cultural worldviews and biases on the text to ensure we truly grasp the message God intended. While we have learned much about these principles, they are always being challenged and refined. Interpretation is both a science and a skill; it is an ongoing challenge.

There are various kinds of errors from mishandling God's Word. Clearly, the most basic problem is communicating false information. Taking truth out of context, misunderstanding the meaning of words and terms, and misinterpreting the intent of the author are various ways that result in error. Jesus's fundamental concern was for those who claimed to speak for God but were intentionally committed to deceive, manipulate, and exploit those to whom they spoke (hence the reference to wolves in sheep's clothing). These prophets were invading the community for their own self-interests regardless of the cost.

One of the greatest stumbling blocks for Israel, outside of simply disobeying God's Word, was listening to false prophets who claimed to speak for God but spoke out of their own imagination rather than passing on the will of the Lord. Fewer things had greater importance than knowing truth from error. The source of truth were prophets who genuinely represented the Lord God. Nothing would be considered a more serious offense than tampering with that truth.

In our world, we have established hermeneutical principles that help treat the text with integrity in order to understand the true meaning of the message. God's revelation in the Law has always been one of the defining differences between God's people and the gods of the other nations. Jesus clearly defended the importance of God's Word when He said that God's people do not live by bread alone, but by every word that proceeds from the mouth of God (Matthew 4:4). In spite of these precautions, false prophets are as real today as they were back in the time of Jesus. If we go back up to the beginning of His Sermon on the Mount, Jesus explains that not the smallest letter or stroke of the Law will pass away until all has been fulfilled (Matthew 5:17-20). God's Word is of supreme importance to Jesus and will be to all who follow Him.

THE AUTHORITY OF GOD'S WORD

The constant problem of understanding a culture so foreign to our own makes understanding the intent of the author especially challenging. Assuming the first-century culture saw the world differently from modern-day America may seem obvious, but imposing our own worldview on the text is a very real and subtle danger. This, combined with cultural pressures to reinterpret the Bible, provides a constant challenge to make the exercise of interpretation a sobering and serious endeavor. Others are relying on pastoral credibility and faithfulness to share the Word of God with the highest level of integrity. This is the most fundamental and demanding principle we keep at the forefront of our mind.

We are handling God's Word, not just the thoughts and imaginations of men. This revelation, given by God Himself, is delivered by the Holy Spirit, the Divine Author who chose human messengers to transmit the heart of God to a broken and lost world. This Word stands outside the corruption of a world damaged by sin and evil. This Bible is the inerrant and infallible Word of God (2 Timothy 3:16-17).

This is a never-ending burden for teachers, pastors, professors, and anyone who teaches the truth of God's Word. This concern is shared by Sunday School teachers, youth workers, and Bible study leaders. The issue is not just about teaching truth but a battle for the nature of truth.

Living in a world that has abandoned objective truth, the door has been opened to doubt the reliability of God's Word. Our culture challenges that this revelation is both infallible and inerrant. Unfortunately, there are many who claim to know Christ who are also reinterpreting the text in ways that fit with needs. We would expect this from a world that has never submitted to God's authority, but it is a constant challenge even in the sphere of the community of faith. Most are very sincere, but some are seeking to exploit God's Word to take advantage of God's people.

COMPROMISING TRUTH

The devil was and continues to be, the greatest of all false prophets. From the beginning of time, his mission has been to cast aspersions on God's Word. His tactic to lure Adam and Eve to disobey the Lord was to get them to question the reliability of God's communicated word. Through careful manipulation, he created enough doubt in Eve's mind to question her understanding of God's Word. Their error was the demise of all humanity. Jesus describes Satan as a murderer and one who does not stand in truth. He is the father of lies because it is his very nature (John 8:44).

It is no surprise that the devil used similar tactics to tempt Jesus when he tried to bribe the Son to abandon the will of the Father and serve His own purposes. Two inseparable issues consistently surfaced with his temptations and certainly were at stake during Jesus's temptation: His faithfulness to His Father and compromising the Word of God.

As a result, we tend to think of temptation in one-dimensional terms. Some evil thing or entity lures God's people away from God and from doing His will; essentially, that is true. But evil in and of itself would be easy to reject if seen for what it really was – evil! The problem with temptation is that evil disguises itself as something good; otherwise, the power of temptation will vanish. The very nature of false prophets is that they are people who appear to be prophets sent by God but are not. Temptation reaches the peak of its power when disguised as something good. When the devil tempted Jesus, he even used the Scriptures to provoke Jesus to prove that the Father would keep His promises. The most subtle and most dangerous temptations are often grounded in Scriptures to lure people away from their faith in the Father.

Unfortunately, the collateral damage of similar deception has affected countless lives. Faith has been decimated in the face of the irreconcilable dilemma of placing too much confidence in people rather than in God's Word. This is even more complicated when deceptive people prey on the trust of those who are convinced they are messengers of God.

Consequently, when a person becomes a victim of such falsehood, everything about God's promises appears to be hollow and empty. Instead of placing their belief in God and their faith in His promises, they inadvertently transferred their faith to a finite person claiming to represent Him. Instead of diligently seeking God in light of human betrayal, many end up deconstructing their faith and walking away from the church and sometimes their faith. They have allowed people to destroy their relationship with the Father.

When confidence in God has been broken, the desire for the Body of Christ is crushed, and the desire for God's purpose disappears. When all is said and done, false prophets, teachers, and apostles are instruments of the devil whom he uses to tempt God's children to alter the trajectory of their lives away from God.

Unfortunately, the all-too-common solution to such disappointment has been to dismiss the church, divorce from the community of faith, and find more utilitarian approaches to deal with the issues and concerns of life. Some hang on to their faith and keep it personal but avoid all who have left a bad spiritual taste in their mouth. Others exchange the truth about God for their own wisdom, and having abandoned the true God, they worship the creation rather than the Creator (Romans 1:25).

DISTORTING TRUTH

The idea that God's Word was the means by which the devil tempted Jesus sounds absurd, and yet this was his camouflage for evil. Certainly, God's Word has often become the pivot point of the rise and fall of God's people from the beginning of their existence. God's Word has been the centerpiece of conflict and controversy to know His blessing or His curse. Obedience brought blessing, and disobedience brought discipline. All these things pivot around their posture before God's Word.

The devil distorts God's Word in the minds of God's people by taking truth out of context, misapplying principles, misrepresenting God's intent, rejecting His will, or neglecting its wisdom. His goal is to deflect His people off the narrow pathway to embrace the wide path of human ingenuity.

Compromising God's Word has been the fundamental downfall for God's people throughout Biblical history. Disobedience to the commands of God has been an ongoing stumbling block for His people, from preventing His people from entering the Promised Land to chasing after the gods of the surrounding nations.

Where Israel failed, Jesus was faithful. While Israel tried to create their own path, Christ remained faithful. The comparison was never coincidental. Christ was faithful to God's will, and He was loyal to the path the Father called Him to walk.

The unique nature of Jesus's warning about false prophets was not a new thing in Israel, but it gained a new level of acceptability. The Pharisees and Scribes had mastered the role of being false prophets even though they were the lay nobility; they were the community leaders of Israel. They were not clergy or what one might consider the spiritual leaders of Israel; that role belonged to the High Priest, the collective of chief priests, and the Levites. But Jesus's harshest judgment was levied against the Pharisees and Scribes.

To understand the wider implications of false prophets that Jesus warned about in Matthew 7, it is helpful to see both the historical context of false messengers and the reality of what Jesus had to deal with in Israel. This scenario was the same warning Moses made to the people of Israel back in Deuteronomy 13:

"If a prophet or a dreamer of dreams arises among you and gives you a sign or a wonder, and the sign or wonder that he tells you comes to pass, and if he says, 'Let us go after other gods,' which you have not known, 'and let us serve them,' you shall not listen to the words of that prophet or that dreamer of dreams. For the Lord your God is testing you, to know whether you love the Lord your God with all your heart and with all your soul. You shall walk after the Lord your God and fear him and keep his commandments and obey his voice, and you shall serve him and hold fast to him."

Deuteronomy 13:1-4

False prophets typically arose from the midst of the people of God, even though pagan nations also had diviners and prophets, too. While every warning about false teachers extended to foreign messengers, the fact that many false teachers rose up from within Israel made this temptation all the more dangerous. Hearing from people within the community who had new insight into God's will could be very compelling. They were people they already trusted; they had history together and had often shared experiences. False prophets claimed to speak for God, so their voices would carry more weight than normal. Moses warned that these false prophets may have every appearance to be genuine. Their claim to speak for God was supplemented by providing some sign that validated their truth claim. They were persuasive, compelling, and powerful in their message; they spoke with authority.

Yet, in spite of all these outward affirmations, the deciding factor of whether they were false prophets was if they led God's people away from the Lord to serve other gods. Regardless of their claim, any sign or wonder, no matter how persuasive they were, if they caused God's people to move away from being loyal to God or obedience to His Word, this alone would prove they were false prophets.

GOD TESTING HIS PEOPLE

What is intriguing about Moses's warnings is that God allowed false prophets to exist in their midst to test His people to see what was in their heart. The concept of testing has several nuances. It can carry the simple idea of a trial, but it can also mean to give experience or train. God's purpose was not to see His people fail; He permitted these experiences to give His people the opportunity to demonstrate their love for Him. In the face of real temptation, the Lord was training them to demonstrate faithfulness to Him, to walk in His ways, fear Him, keep His commandments, and obey His voice. They had a wonderful, albeit strenuous, opportunity to demonstrate the quality of their relationship with the Lord by choosing to serve and hold fast to *Him* (Deuteronomy 13:1-4).

The severity of their circumstances had no bearing on whether the Lord was with them or not. He was always present with His people, and He had His fingerprints on every aspect of their journey. While it was hard for them to recognize the invisible movements of the Lord in the face of physical trials and emotional hardships, the Lord was actively engaged with His people. He desired to know the spiritual condition of His people's hearts and, at the same time, provide an occasion for faith.

In this sense, the Lord led them into a situation to perfect their faith and deepen their relationship with Him. In the crucible of real life, and certainly from the finite human perspective, this will always appear uncertain and risky. But in the heart of Israel's God, He was training His people for godliness.

One might speculate these temptations could have resulted in evil, but it was always intended by God to validate their love and cultivate faith. Whatever language you utilize, God allowed, permitted, or brought His people face to face with a serious temptation for the purpose of testing them. He wanted to see what was in their heart and to strengthen their faith and confidence in Him as the one true God.

THE ENEMY AMONGST US

Facing this kind of temptation became even more sobering when the prophet or dreamer was one of their family members:

> "If your brother, the son of your mother, or your son or your daughter or the wife you embrace or your friend who is as your own soul entices you secretly, saying, 'Let us go and serve other gods,' which neither you nor your fathers have known, some of the gods of the peoples who are around you, whether near you or far off from you, from the one end of the earth to the other, you shall not yield to him or listen to him, nor shall your eye pity

him, nor shall you spare him, nor shall you conceal him. But you shall kill him. Your hand shall be first against him to put him to death, and afterward the hand of all the people. You shall stone him to death with stones because he sought to draw you away from the Lord your God, who brought you out of the land of Egypt, out of the house of slavery. And all Israel shall hear and fear and never again do any such wickedness as this among you."

Deuteronomy 13:6-11

We tend to think of prophets as a formal role – those officially chosen by God who speak on God's behalf. This text does not label family members as false prophets, but the defining characteristics that essentially identify a false prophet, leading God's people to serve other gods, was exactly the concern about an ordinary person in the community advocating the same departure from God's Word.

It is clear from this text that sometimes the most dangerous temptations are hidden in plain sight: family. The power of human influence, especially from close family or friends, was one of the most dangerous temptations Israel would ever face. No other temptation would be more compelling than when a family member who, for any reason, tried to convince his family to pursue other gods. Regardless of the justification, the result was a betrayal to their heavenly Father. The punishment, as severe as it is, indicates how seriously God places on being faithful to Him and His Word, even above being loyal to family.

Family dynamics have always been a powerful leverage that the devil has exploited to divide families and create disunity. The very nature of living in a world damaged by evil and sin originated with the deception of Adam and Eve. Their sin impacted their relationship and their sons, resulting in jealousy, disappointment, and murder. While it might be hard to measure how much influence the devil has had in the hearts of our family members, the deterioration and destruction of the family through human history is, arguably, catastrophic. False truth, distrust, deception, and many more things have been the pitfalls that have torn the family apart.

Children who rebel against their parents and their faith have caused extreme distress in families. Parents question their ability to raise their kids, and children often blame their parents for how they were raised. Some families have been resilient to the voices in the world, while others have disintegrated under the weight of the world. No parent is perfect, and no child will ever grow up where they won't have to forgive his or her parents for something. Regardless of the reason is described as hypocrisy, legalism, or deception, the perception that people were inauthentic can result in some family members discarding their faith under false pretenses.

THE MESSAGE BEFORE THE MESSENGER

From a historical perspective, the simplest way to interpret a false prophet is anything that diverged from God's Word. Obviously, their claim to speak for God needs to be authenticated so others know the messages are genuine. Certainly, their word must match God's revelation, and the first line of examination is that their message needed to correspond with God's truth. Understanding the nuances and accuracy of doctrine and correct theology is an obvious starting place.

However, the way Jesus taught His disciples to vet the true nature of the messenger is by the fruit of their lives (Matthew 7:15). Jesus introduced His men to the concept that actions speak louder than words, but character brings clarity to true nature. Jesus did not define specifics regarding the nature of the fruit. His illustration of good and bad trees indicated that, like a tree that produced fruit, so humans produce something out of their life that is either good and healthy or bad and unhealthy:

"Then Jesus said to the crowds and to his disciples, "The scribes and the Pharisees sit on Moses' seat, so do and observe whatever they tell you, but not the works they do. For they preach, but do not practice. They tie up heavy burdens, hard to bear, and lay them on people's shoulders, but they themselves are not willing to move them with their finger. They do all their deeds to be seen by others. For they make their phylacteries broad and their fringes long."

Matthew 23:1-5.

First, since the Pharisees and Scribes had positions of authority, Jesus told people to do what they said but not what they did. The Pharisees and Scribes were self-proclaimed experts of the Law. They were not an authority unto themselves; they sat in the seat of Moses, indicating that the Law given by God was supposed to be the final authority. Jesus condemned their unwillingness to submit to the very Law they proclaimed to others.

Regardless of whether one labels this as hypocrisy or false teaching, the defining characteristic of both is that they taught the truth but exempted themselves from obeying the very truth they taught. They sounded authentic, but the fruit of their life betrayed their teaching. The exhortation is to not do what the hypocrites do. The fruit of their life betrayed what they taught even though they spoke the truth. The problem with false teachers is the deception that they have the right to tell everyone else how to live but do not abide by their own teaching.

Jesus clearly indicated that a discerning ear hears truth regardless of the messenger. When the message is true, it needs to be heard and obeyed, even if the messengers are hypocrites. His disciples were encouraged to resist the temptation to use the hypocrisy of others as their own personal excuse to not obey the truth themselves. Blaming others for their own lack of obedience would be the posture of the naïve and immature. Mature disciples are motivated by a desire to honor their heavenly Father, not reacting to the failures of other humans.

Secondly, false teachers make demands on others but do nothing to help them with their spiritual responsibilities. Jesus warned that false teachers are like ravenous wolves. They levy demands and expectations on others to control them and set their own standard for spirituality, all the while imposing their personal convictions on others. They weaponize their convictions against others to control and manipulate.

The nature of false prophets does little to nothing to help others enter the kingdom. They are more concerned about doing everything to impress people with their power and position. Truth that does not transform discredits the messenger and undermines truth. Teaching truths that are not applied by the one who is communicating that truth leaves a spiritual vacancy and void. Jesus pointed out that grapes do not come from thorn bushes in the same way that figs are not produced from thorn bushes. Good trees produce good fruit, and bad trees produce bad fruit. If a tree produces bad fruit, it is of no value except to be cut down and thrown away.

GOD IS THE EXPERT

We live in a world where everyone claims to be an expert, and every conceivable avenue of communication boasts a myriad of voices providing wisdom for life. Many of these are helpful, but there are many that do not match God's Word because they call individuals to be masters of their own fate and champion their own destiny. While many have their place, there are voices everywhere speaking lies and deception – the world is filled with false prophets.

The concept of our heavenly Father leading His children into temptation has another side than just exposing His children to a test. If our heavenly Father leads us to a test, it is also a promise of His personal presence in facing that trial. His provision sustains and guides us when facing temptation. The Lord never leaves or abandons us amid a trial, test, or temptation. The personal presence of our heavenly Father is His promise, just like the Spirit of God was with Jesus in the wilderness.

False prophets always camouflage their presence. Disguise and deceit are cloaked with good intentions. The apostle Paul made the same argument with the Corinthians:

> "And what I am doing I will continue to do, in order to undermine the claim of those who would like to claim that in their boasted mission they work on the same terms as we do. For such men are false apostles, deceitful workmen, disguising themselves as apostles of Christ. And no wonder, for even Satan disguises himself as an angel of light. So it is no surprise if his servants, also, disguise themselves as servants of righteousness. Their end will correspond to their deeds."
>
> 2 Corinthians 11:12-15

Messengers of Satan, regardless of title or role, ultimately imitate the one they serve. Satan disguised himself as an angel of light, and those who serve him do the same. They pretend to serve Christ but secretly oppose Him, which makes discerning truth very challenging. Since humanity has been infected by sin and damaged by evil, people do not need the devil's help in being deceptive, manipulative, or controlling. Yet, these behaviors are clearly representative of the activity of the devil to lure God's people from remaining faithful to their heavenly Father.

Part of the purpose of the Lord leading His children into any context to face testing, and more specifically temptation, is to train them to resist the devil and learn to trust the Lord. The objective of this training is not just to pass the test but to be equipped to help others who face, or will face, the same temptation in life. Those who are trained by these experiences learn to discern the subtle schemes of the devil, to recognize how he conceals himself and his messengers. They have their senses trained to discern the difference between good and evil. They learn through those tests and temptations to pass on the wisdom of God to those who are young and naïve. They learn to selflessly care for others and provide divine perspective and the mind of Christ related to avoiding spiritual landmines and relational pitfalls.

Those who are led into temptation learn to embrace the character of their heavenly Father in the face of extreme testing. They learn godliness in the face of evil and learn to make faith choices when circumstances provoke them to do otherwise. Their faith matures and refines in the crucible of a fallen world. Godliness deepens through the trial of temptation. These temptations equip the children of God to serve His kingdom purpose.

It would be foolish for God to overprotect His children to the extent that they spend much of their lives shielded from every harm and the presence of evil, isolated from the affliction of a broken world held captive by the evil one. This would hardly show the strength of the Father's grace and love for sinful human beings if He can redeem them but could not empower them to live godly lives in a broken world.

The apostle Paul understood the nature of temptation. His thoughts align with the heart of Jesus as He taught the Corinthians the nature of God's provision in the face of such temptation:

"No temptation has overtaken you that is not common to man. God is faithful, and he will not let you be tempted beyond your ability, but with the temptation he will also provide the way of escape, that you may be able to endure it."

1 Corinthians 10:13

Regardless of how overwhelming any given situation is, God is faithful to His children. He always has been faithful, and He always will be faithful. He faithfully provides a way of escape, a means to find a way through the danger, but there has always been a faith component to overcoming tests or temptation. The child of God must learn to live by faith, not by sight, to fight the worldly forces of darkness and the spiritual forces in heavenly places.

PRINCIPLES IN DEALING WITH THE TEMPTATION OF FALSE PROPHETS:

1. Our heavenly Father can lead His children into testing, which may include temptation, to empower them in their relationship with Him and equip them to serve His kingdom purpose.

   - How has God used temptations to deepen your love for Him?
   - What have you learned about your relationship with the Father when facing temptations?

2. Our heavenly Father cannot be tempted by evil, and He himself does not tempt anyone, but He may seek to demonstrate the power of His grace and the character of His children by permitting the devil to tempt His children.

   - How do you think through the idea that God uses Satan to test His children?
   - What temptations have God the Father provided a way of escape for you?
   - What have you learned about the power of His presence in temptations?

3. There will always be false prophets and hypocrites, but God will often use these to train His children to resist temptation from the evil one to embrace kingdom values and priorities.

   - How have you recognized the Father's hand in your life when you have been confronted by false truth?
   - How do you recognize the difference between Satan and the Father when you face trials and temptations?

4. Regardless of how we often feel, our heavenly Father has His fingerprints on our lives and is always with His children. The

power of His personal presence is our greatest resource for resisting temptation and choosing faith instead of fear.

- How do you keep from treating God as an idea instead of being a real person?
- What things do you do to keep from taking Christ for granted?

PRAYER

Heavenly Father, teach me to trust you as the author and perfecter of my faith. Thank you that you work all things, including trials and temptations, ultimately for my good. You desire to cultivate Christ in me and equip me to serve you in your kingdom work here on earth. We live in a world that has been damaged by sin and evil, and you, in your kindness, continue to train me to deal with such temptations and trials so I might serve others by showing your grace and kindness will always be sufficient for every circumstance of life.

Teach me not to allow false teachers and hypocrites to harden my heart to a genuine relationship with you. Help my faith cling to you and embrace your truth regardless of the brokenness that surrounds me. Help me to live out of the fullness of your presence in me and not allow myself to become entrapped by the chaos and confusion in others. Help me to move alongside others with grace and truth to help them see the freedom they can experience in Christ.

Lord, help me realize that I alone am accountable to you for my walk with you. In your kindness, you have provided other believers from whom I can learn to imitate their faith. You have redeemed people from all walks of life and built your church. They are your gifts to me to help me grow my faith and serve your purpose. Guard my heart to refrain from blaming others for my own unbelief. Amen.

CHAPTER 9

STOP PERFORMING, START LIVING

Escaping the Pressure to Put on a Show

"Not everyone who says to me, 'Lord, Lord', will enter the kingdom of heaven, but the one who does the will of my Father who is in heaven. On that day many will say to me, 'Lord, Lord did we not prophecy in your name, and cast out demons in your name, and do many mighty works in your name?

And then I will declare to them, I never knew you; depart from me, you workers of lawlessness."

Matthew 7:15-23

I remember that when our son Ryan was in junior high, he was uncertain if he wanted to play baseball or lacrosse. Lacrosse had just begun to grow as a community sport and was spreading rapidly. It was getting pretty late to register for baseball, and he was not confident about playing, but he had not decided what he wanted to do.

Part of his hesitation was not being sure if he would get on the ball team with his friends whom he had played with for years, and he was starting to lose interest in baseball. In all of this uncertainty, we received a call from one of the coaches who helped coordinate the league. He asked to come over and talk with Ryan. When he arrived, he asked if Ryan wanted to play for their team because there was a great need for players, and he needed Ryan.

He ended up convincing Ryan to play. They got back to us after a couple of days with all the right forms, schedules, and team assignments, which also indicated the team on which Ryan had been placed. But to Ryan's distress, the coach placed him on a different team from what he had promised when he met with him. Ryan was convinced that the coach was recruiting him for his own team, but he was placed with a team where he did not even know the coach or any of the players!

Ryan immediately deflated; he was so disheartened that he immediately blurted out that he was not going to play. He felt deceived because both of us were under the impression the coach was recruiting Ryan for his own team, not someone else's team. Ryan felt betrayed, even though it might be better to describe this as a misunderstanding rather than intentional deception. When I called the coach and told him, he explained he was recruiting for the league and not his personal team; they had filled their roster much earlier. Either way, what we thought was going to happen turned out very differently, and the result was that our son jumped from baseball to lacrosse.

The final temptation was a form of self-deception. Our initial reaction will shock us at first glance. Individuals fervently committed to serving the Lord here on earth may come to find out that they are rejected by the very one whom they claim to serve.

This has become one of the most disturbing and sobering texts in all the Scriptures. It is deeply unsettling to many Christians because of the very nature of those who appear to be faithful servants who are ultimately rejected. Their conviction seemed unabated, but in reality, their claim was not validated when they were face to face with Jesus.

These events certainly raise some lingering doubts and concerns for anyone who reads this narrative. The obvious question is, "How could this happen and why?" Are these individuals true believers who somehow lost their salvation, or are they pretenders who, in spite of outward appearances, never possessed a genuine faith that truly embraced the reality of Christ? The nature of this text has disturbed Christians for centuries, and there does not seem to be an adequate resolution to the nature of these particular verses.

SERVING GOD OR KNOWING HIM

The outcome of a life of spiritual service that ends in rejection appears harsh. These individuals had every expectation they were doing everything right. They were, in their own mind, committed to doing the Lord's work here on earth. All three activities mentioned would appear to have a divine fingerprint upon them, which, by their very nature, affirms the Lord's presence and power.

The critical concern of this text hinges on who has the right to enter the kingdom of heaven. This adds even more confusion to the text since these people were clearly committed to activities that no one would question if they were aligned with the Lord's kingdom work on earth.

The dilemma of serving the Lord and then being disqualified by Him ought to raise deep concerns over the expectations and qualifications required to enter that kingdom. You do not want to fall into the category of believing that you serve the Lord, maybe for your whole life, and then discover you are not qualified to enter the very kingdom you proclaimed.

We know from an earlier text that Jesus came calling Israel to repent "for the kingdom of heaven is at hand" (Matthew 4:17). Israel needed to repent to enter and enjoy the privilege of entering. Their current spiritual condition, their heritage, their Jewish tradition, and their practices did not qualify them to enter the kingdom. They had either never qualified or lost their way.

In the mind of the Jews, this concept of the kingdom of heaven would be tied to King David's kingdom, but they anticipated a kingdom that would fulfill and reflect the fullness of God's divine glory. Even when Jesus was getting ready to return to the Father, His own disciples were curious if this was the moment in time when Jesus would restore the kingdom of Israel (Acts 1:6).

The problem, however, was that Israel was still not properly reconciled to God's anointed representative, His One and only Son. So, the fulfillment of those historical promises would take a different timeline as God would now offer the opportunity to enter this kingdom to the Gentiles.

WHAT DOES IT TAKE TO ENTER THE KINGDOM

From a New Covenant perspective, the issue would also center in the person of Jesus. We know that when any individual responds to the gospel and the death and resurrection of Christ, they are delivered from the dominion of darkness and transferred into the kingdom of His beloved Son (Colossians 1:13). The common denominator that runs through the gospel proclaimed to Israel and the New Testament gospel is the person of Christ.

Entering the kingdom of heaven is equivalent to our concept of eternal life. God promised David His descendant, ultimately Christ Himself, would rule this kingdom forever. The promise of Christ in the New Testament, grounded in the death and resurrection of Jesus, is eternal life. The qualification for entering that kingdom is anchored to responding to the good news that being reconciled with the Father is only through faith in Christ. He is the defining and final authority as to who enters the kingdom of heaven.

When we come back to Matthew 7:22-23, these people stood before the Lord confident of their own faithfulness to Him. The Lord's response is shocking! He announces that these very people would not enter the kingdom. Regardless of their argument advocating their faithfulness to Jesus by their works, the final authority is in the power of Jesus. In this text, Jesus made a judgment, not based on their activity, but upon His own insight, that He never knew them and commanded them to depart from Him. The demise of these individuals appeared completely unfair and confusing. Consequently, it would be worth briefly exploring why these activities were not sufficient evidence to validate their claim.

There were three kinds of activities these individuals were deeply committed to carrying out to serve the Lord: prophecy, casting out demons, and miracles. What complicated the performance of these activities even more was they did all these things "in His name." The deception was rooted in a false claim. "Not everyone who says to me (Jesus), Lord, Lord will enter the kingdom of God."

RESUME OR RELATIONSHIP

Jesus's rejection of these people brings these temptations back into the context of things that will keep individuals out of the future fulfillment of the kingdom of heaven. If these individuals actually believe that they knew the Lord or they think good works are sufficient to convince Jesus that they were good enough, we are not told. In the language of Jesus, they have not entered the narrow gate, so their claim to know Him falls on deaf ears.

Their resume of services offered to Jesus is impressive. They claimed to do three things: they prophesied in His name, they cast out demons in His name, and they did mighty works in His name. These three have particular importance in Jesus's commentary, especially related to the prayer asking Him not to lead them into temptation.

These people claimed to prophesy in His name. The basic concept of prophesying is proclaiming God's Word. One aspect of prophesying is simply speaking forth God's Word. It is making a declaration from God on His behalf, speaking His truth into the life experience of the community. Arguably, there are different expressions of prophecy, including preaching, teaching, declaration, and proclaiming the gospel to a lost world.

The other dimension of prophecy is predicting the future. More than a quarter of the Scriptures are devoted to speaking into the future events from the point of view of the speaker. Prophetic Scripture reveals the sovereignty of God as He reveals how He will place His fingerprints on the unfolding events in the future.

The text does not reveal the scope of their prophetic ministry, but we can acknowledge it could include a wide range of contexts and expressions. The inevitable conundrum is that prophecy would infer divine empowerment from the Spirit of God, who is always present to empower true prophets to speak on God's behalf (2 Peter 1:20-21).

While some of these voices would have included the false prophets mentioned earlier, this list goes beyond just prophecy to include a broader range of spiritual activity, such as having the power to cast out demons which would demonstrate power over the evil one and his cohort of spiritual forces of wickedness. Performing miracles most likely speaks to healing and helping the most vulnerable.

They also declared to have cast out demons in Jesus' name. The picture they painted was going to battle with the evil one and His cohort and triumphing over them. There was no corroborating evidence other than their claim. While this could be true, and there may be no reason to doubt it, this may also border on wishful thinking based on a commitment to fighting evil in the world and projecting their efforts to an exaggerated level to be equivalent to casting out the enemy.

Finally, they performed miracles in Jesus's name. The language suggests powerful works with the assumption that they are being done by the power of God. All three were done as if to impress Jesus with all they had done for Him.

CHRIST'S CRITERIA TO ENTER THE KINGDOM

Regardless of whether these claims are true or only true in their own minds, Jesus does not spend time exploring or debating the validity of these claims. There were two standards by which Jesus identified that were not being met by these individuals. These two criteria are obviously those things that Jesus was looking for, and He did not find them present in the lives of these people.

The first criteria was doing the will of the Father who was in heaven. What was deeply disturbing was Jesus leaned into this discussion by indicating that not everyone who says to Him, "Lord, Lord," will enter the kingdom. There was a clear disconnect between what these individuals claimed and what was actually true. You might argue, how can prophesying, casting out demons, and doing miracles not be doing God's will? That would seem preposterous.

Israel's history would argue differently. When God called Moses to lead Israel out of Egypt, Pharaoh's magicians replicated the miracles that Aaron performed. While they could not reproduce all the miracles, they did a pretty good job keeping up for a time. Yet the reality would point to the fact that just because they claimed to do these things, and even if they did some of these things, this was not the same as doing His will.

When you read Matthew 24:23-24, Jesus pointed out that there will be many who will appear, claiming to be Christ. Many false prophets will also arise and will show great signs and wonders so as to mislead, if possible, even the elect. Apparently, Satan and his forces can do these same kinds of activities, and in and of themselves do not guarantee the handiwork of God. While it is obvious that both Jesus and the disciples did these very same things in their ministry to Israel, these stand-alone activities were not sufficient to guarantee entrance into the kingdom of heaven.

In order for us to broaden our perspective even more, we need to realize there is another caveat to these gifts and powers these so-called-disciples apparently did not understand. Jesus's admonition to the 70 He sent to prepare Israel for His coming is striking. These disciples were ecstatic because they had the power to overcome Satan. Nothing could hurt them, and they had the authority to cast out demons. Jesus challenged their enthusiasm and redirected their focus. Instead of rejoicing in having the power to do miraculous works, He encouraged them to rejoice that their names were written in heaven (Luke 10:17-20).

The central issue for the Lord was not if they claimed to know Him but if He actually knew them. Jesus rejected them because He never knew them. The grammar is indefinite, so the implication is that Jesus had never actually known them in a redemptive, familial manner; they were not part of God's family. This was virtually the same line of thought Paul had when writing to the Galatians.

> "Formerly, when you did not know God, you were enslaved to those that by nature are not gods. But now that you have come to know God, or rather to be known by God, how can you turn back again to the weak and worthless elementary principles of the world, whose slaves you want to be once more?"
>
> Galatians 4:8-9

The idea of not knowing God, or not having been known by God, is a clear reference to those who were not in a familial relationship with Him. In each case, the difference between unsaved or being saved was if they were known by God.

The Lord's rejection of these individuals was grounded on the fact that Jesus did not know them and commanded them to depart (Matthew 7:23). His charge was they were workers of lawlessness. Since no information enlightens us as to what that means, you can know that whatever good things they "did for Jesus" were not adequate to offset their works of lawlessness, even if that could influence the outcome.

GETTING BACK TO THE ESSENTIALS

Doing works for God does not precede knowing Him. Paul made abundantly clear that a person is not justified before God by works of the law; he or she is justified by faith (Romans 3:27). The claim to believe in God resulting in doing works for God did not matter to Jesus when He announced that He did not know these people. Religion often advocates good works to validate our claim of believing in God. Jesus made it clear the only works that flow out of the reality that Jesus knows them validated any claim to serve Him.

Even more importantly, if you read back through the Lord's Prayer, not one of these activities is mentioned as critical to following the narrow pathway. The substance of the Lord's Prayer did not speak to prophecy, nor to casting out demons, and nor about doing miracles. Jesus did not even mention these as He laid out this spiritual blueprint for a God-honoring life.

As much as we often rely on these things, they are not indispensable to a Spirit-filled, God-honoring life. They are not critical to commending us to the Lord; neither would neglecting them, unless, as with the disciples, it was part of an assignment.

The challenge for everyone is to determine what kinds of practices, giftedness, and experiences are truly indispensable to your walk with Christ and what things might be desirable and others optional. If we confuse the essential with what is helpful, then we will be out of sync with Christ's blueprint for life.

MASTERING THE MAIN THINGS

Some might argue there are all kinds of things that Jesus did not talk about in His prayer that are mentioned in the New Testament writings that are important: spiritual gifts, spiritual leadership, the nature of the Body of Christ, and a host of other important topics. That, of course, is very true, but you have to remember why Jesus taught His disciples this prayer. He was helping them understand the absolute essentials to overcome the spiritual landmines and relational pitfalls in this world, in order to live a Spirit-filled, God-honoring life.

There are lots of important things that believers or disciples need to learn in their walk with God, but if they do not understand and master this foundational blueprint, they may replace what is essential with things that are simply helpful. Neglecting the essentials to become masters of what is helpful will ultimately undermine our own walk with our heavenly Father. In this case, this becomes the difference between actually knowing Christ and not entering His kingdom.

Regardless, Jesus did not interrogate their claim or discredit it. In fact, Jesus did not address these particular claims at all. Even though, in their minds, these services were all done to portray allegiance to Jesus, He simply ignored these claims. Instead, He declared that He did not know any of them.

We are suddenly confronted with a tricky, sobering truth. People can call Jesus Lord, believe they have spent their life serving Him, fighting the evil in this world, and even helping those most vulnerable, and still not be in a right relationship with Christ. This was not just a problem of being out of fellowship with Him, which is easily overcome through confession and restoration, but this can result in the ultimate despair of permanent separation from His presence.

This raises a modern-day dilemma that requires some reflection. The obvious context that may be the most beneficial for every believer may also create the most vulnerability. Families who grow up in the church are exposed to the most generous gift of God's grace, the fellowship of a faith community, and the nurturing of the church. Kids raised up in the church are exposed to His truth, a community that worships and serves the Lord.

The greatest temptation the community of faith must face is surrounding our kids with everything they need but never creating a culture that allows them to embrace Christ. Churches have programs, ministries, activities, events, conferences, service projects, Sunday school classes, and holiday services. We spend endless hours teaching the Bible, going on mission trips, taking spiritual gift surveys, and so forth.

Unless every person understands their personal responsibility for their own spiritual welfare, people may learn to comply with church customs and practices but never grasp what it means to know Christ. Activities do not guarantee genuine faith; they only provide the *opportunity* for faith. Faith is not something others do for us; faith is something we exercise for ourselves. Nothing we do guarantees faith for our kids.

CHURCH PRACTICES AND TRADITIONS

Churches have their own distinctive practices, from membership requirements to leadership qualifications to church ordinances. Most evangelical churches practice the Lord's Supper and various forms of baptism. But these practices, especially within denominations, can be varied and extremely different. Some have infant baptism, while others practice child dedication, which often have very different purposes. Communion, also known as the Lord's Supper or Eucharist, can cause debates and divisions on how to practice it. Even when practices are similar, there are theological differences in understanding the essential nature of this historical church tradition.

Church traditions are often the foundation of church distinctives, which are the pride and joy of many. Both formal and informal traditions are the fabric of why a church exists, while other traditions have locked some churches into the past with no vision or flexibility to change and grow. Unfortunately, holding to these deeply embedded convictions of how to do church right has often resulted in the death of many churches.

We live in an age where church attendance is dropping across the country. Many have become disillusioned with churches that seem more committed to cultural issues than the gospel. Ideology has divided congregations even to the point of church splits. People have spent half their life in a church environment, and when they suddenly look up and wonder what difference all this has really made on their life.

In spite of our pride over our unique distinctives, we have lost our sense of unity around Christ and the Biblical purpose for why the church was created in the first place. It would seem that we are more concerned about our branding than the work of the kingdom. Instead of living out a dynamic faith, people have started weaponizing their convictions to try and force others to conform to their idea of maturity.

We can debate all day about whose fault it is that people are leaving the church. Those who leave often have superficial reasons, if there are any reasons, and church leadership is often more committed to the status quo than discovering the mind of Christ. On the other hand, people can do very hurtful things to others, which can destroy their faith. They are spiritual victims of spiritual abuse.

Either way, we end up judging each other's spiritual commitment and avoid true spiritual fellowship. The reality may be closer to the idea that everyone has fallen victim to these temptations to one degree or another, and we find our hearts slightly hardened by the deceitfulness of sin.

The temptation of doing good works as a means to gain eternal life has always been the trap of religion. It confuses cause and effect. Good works are to be an expression of the narrow path, but it is not how we are to enter the narrow gate. Relationship with the Father has always been the prerequisite of responsibility. The Bible is clear that salvation from sin is never grounded in good works. No individual can earn God's favor by doing enough things that prove to the Father He should accept them.

Many who have grown up in the church with their programs, practices, policies, and traditions have become so disheartened that they are abandoning church. The obvious concern is that we do not want to raise up people who confess Jesus as Lord and have conformed to our church culture but have not been changed or transformed by the gospel.

One of the dangers of our systems is regardless of our intent, many misunderstand them as creating a performance-based salvation, also known as works-based salvation. This plagues the mindset of individuals and churches. In Matthew 7:21-23 this was exactly the problem. People who claimed to know God but tried to accomplish the kingdom of heaven by works ultimately find out this will never work. Even spiritual activity, no matter how well conformed to these practices, does not qualify a person for the kingdom if unknown to Jesus.

One of the most powerful reminders of this is Colossians 2. People were judging others over questions about food and drink, festivals, and Sabbath days:

> "Therefore let no one pass judgment on you in questions of food and drink, or with regard to a festival or a new moon or a Sabbath. These are a shadow of the things to come, but the substance belongs to Christ."
>
> Colossians 2:16-17

Any kind of spiritual tradition or practice can only, at best, be a shadow of what can only be fulfilled in Christ. When people believe they have become good Christians because they keep certain programs, practices, and traditions, these very things may keep people from Christ. One cannot deny that any of these things provide an occasion to deepen faith, but they can never, in and of themselves, be a means of grace. While every individual is responsible for their own faith, the danger has been that church programs have become more important than people.

I have been asked on numerous occasions if someone has to belong to our church in order to get to heaven or be saved. Can someone only be saved if they go through our church ordinances and customs? The answer is absolutely not. The reason I am convinced of this is ultimately because salvation is in a person, not in church traditions or practices. I am reminded of Jesus' interaction with the Samaritan woman at the well.

The woman perceived Jesus was a prophet, but due to her moral indiscretions and strong ethnic discrimination, she was an outcast. The issue of being allowed to worship came up in their discussion:

> "Our fathers worshiped on this mountain, but you say that in Jerusalem is the place where people ought to worship." Jesus said to her, "Woman, believe me, the hour is coming when neither on this mountain nor in Jerusalem will you worship the Father. You worship what you do not know; we worship what we know, for salvation is from the Jews. But the hour is coming, and is now here, when the true worshipers will worship the Father in spirit and truth, for the Father is seeking such people to worship him. God is spirit, and those who worship him must worship in spirit and truth."
>
> John 4:20-24

This truth is necessary in our modern culture. Worship is not confined to a particular place or practices. True believers worship in spirit and in truth. If churches do not shepherd the hearts of people to understand this fundamental truth, believers worship an institution, not Jesus. True worship is in harmony with the character of our God, and we are in grave danger of raising people who do much for God but do not know Him.

There has been more division, debate, and disunity over the styles of music, instruments, and forms than anything else. Everyone has their preferences, but this has been a typical example of people worshiping the styles of music rather than the Jesus behind the music.

ARE WE HELPING OR HURTING PEOPLE?

Many who are on the broad way may have had help getting there. When the church loses its spiritual moorings, there is grave danger that we unintentionally push people down the wide pathway. Even the best of intentions can create a performance-based salvation that actually keeps people from the kingdom of heaven.

The narrow and broad way, false prophets, and works-based salvation are temptations that do more than just create disunity; they keep people from the kingdom of heaven. These are the critical tests or temptations that don't only affect individuals but can affect the whole community. The Father will lead some into a context where He permits His people to face and experience these temptations directly in order to perfect their faith and character. He trains and equips His children to serve other believers and His kingdom.

PRINCIPLES IN DEALING WITH TEMPTATIONS:

1. God will test or train His people in order to perfect faith and character.

   - Are you convinced that God is shaping your life journey for your good?
   - How do you recognize God's activity in your life, especially during challenges and trials?

2. God cannot be tempted by evil, and He Himself does not tempt anyone. He may permit the devil to be part of a test so that He can use the experience in the life of His children to cultivate godliness and equip His people to serve others and His kingdom.

   - Can you accept that God can use temptations in your life?
   - What experiences have you had in your life that seemed very overwhelming but ultimately changed you for the better?

3. Three critical temptations are pivotal for God's people to address: walking a different pathway other than His kingdom and righteousness, watching out for false prophets who compromise God's Word, and avoiding a performance-based salvation that believes good works will qualify someone for the kingdom of heaven.

   - How do you experience any or all of these temptations in your journey?
   - What perspective has changed for you about these temptations as you get more clarity on what Jesus taught?

4. These temptations are not experiences anyone would choose themselves, and they can be severe enough to change the trajectory of a person's life.

- What kinds of experiences have you had that have changed the trajectory of your life?
- Do you believe these experiences are ultimately good for you or terrible?

5. Churches can create a culture people conform to but may actually keep people from the kingdom of heaven. Leadership must learn to shepherd the heart of Christ's church and prevent them from conforming to programming.

- Do you grow better in your walk with God by being involved in a program or interacting with it?
- What is more meaningful for your personal growth - doing your own thing or having the encouragement of others?

PRAYER

Father, I desire to live a life that truly honors you. I want you to use anything and everything in my life, or all that you bring or permit into my life, to help me genuinely experience your presence and power even in life's harshest realities, including dealing with evil and the evil one, refine and prepare me so that I can cultivate the maturity and wisdom to serve you well.

Help me to see your fingerprints in every situation and circumstance into which you lead me. Help me to understand that nothing touches my life without your supervision, but I always need to make faith choices to navigate every circumstance. Cultivate in my heart a love for you that has the utmost confidence you are working in me for my ultimate good. Amen.

CHAPTER 10

DELIVER US FROM THE CHAOS

Finding Stability When
Life Gets Messy.

"… but deliver us from evil."

Matthew 6:13

"Therefore, everyone who hears these words of Mine, and acts on them, will be like a wise man who built his house on the rock. And the rain fell and the floods came, and the winds blew and slammed against that house; and yet it did not fall, for it had been founded on the rock."

Matthew 7:24-25.

My first summer after high school, I signed up for a 100-mile canoe trip for two weeks. Twenty students and four adult leaders ventured into the backwoods and lakes of northern Saskatchewan, several of whom had never done anything like this before. The director, a large, stately gentleman, methodically walked us through a number of rules that would keep us safe in this wilderness adventure. The rules were for our protection and for his sanity since he was entrusted with these teenagers for the next couple of weeks. Accidents were always possible, but his guidelines limited unnecessary misadventures that could jeopardize the trip. Any injury or sickness forced difficult choices, but he made it clear that he would not hesitate to send anyone back home if their health or safety was at risk. Any deliberate disobedience to his rules could mean being sent back home with one of the adult leaders, a huge embarrassment to those who felt like doing their own thing. These rules elevated the group needs above individual preferences. Being out in the wilderness required the group to work together. There was no place for lone rangers running off to do their own thing.

Sticking together helped everyone be successful. He assigned each of us a partner with whom we canoed and traversed the portages. We were responsible for each other. We shared a tent, helped each other pack and portage, and kept watch for each other if we started feeling sick. We could not do this alone, and he trained us to work together. Since we were out in the backwaters of Northern Saskatchewan, we had to stay healthy, so he required us to take lake baths at least every other day. The water was very cold, and it was tough to jump in and get clean, but it was necessary. One particular rule was non-negotiable. He created a boundary of several feet around the outdoor cooking site he set up each night. He was adamant that no one was allowed to go near his kitchen, and he never wanted to catch anyone around the stove. Clearly, this was for our protection, as he did not need anyone getting burned when he had the fires going to cook our meals.

One evening, right after dinner, he engaged everyone in a game of "scramble." It essentially amounted to a large candy toss. He threw out all kinds of candy all through the campsite, and some of it fell behind the kitchen. Almost everyone forgot the rules and scrambled all over the camp to grab candy, even behind the kitchen. I took a half step toward the kitchen to grab as much candy as possible but suddenly stopped, looked over at our director, and caught his eye. His look immediately ignited a remembrance of the safety protocols that brought me to a jarring halt just as I was about to dive behind the kitchen to grab my treasure. It was painfully tempting to do what everyone else was doing, but I slowly backed away and went to other places to grab candy.

To my surprise, at the end of our two-week excursion, he commended me in front of the whole group for following the rules, especially the one about not encroaching on the kitchen area. He appreciated the fact that I listened to him and kept his rules even when everyone else forgot. He was not chastising the others for forgetting his rules as much as commending me for remembering and doing what he asked. I never forgot how valued I felt when I respected his requests.

The disciples of Jesus needed to develop a keen awareness of their most powerful spiritual enemy: the devil. He was not some trivial inconvenience, nor was he a figment of their imagination. Outside of their heavenly Father, Satan was the most powerful being they would ever face. He is the god of the world, and the whole world lies under his pervasive influence. He has the power of death, and he is bent to do everything to destroy the work of the Father. The devil attacked Jesus in the wilderness, so there is no reason to think he would hesitate to attack His followers.

Jesus used the prayer to empower His team. They had to learn to work together and support one another in light of the mission of

Christ's kingdom. Jesus knew they could not do this alone, so He trained them to work together. Every pronoun in the Lord's Prayer is a plural pronoun. This meant that the prayer was for everyone in the community and the responsibility of the entire cohort of disciples. This request, asking the Father to deliver them from evil, was obviously for their protection. There was no greater enemy they would face in life and ministry than the evil one. A lack of knowledge of their adversary would foolishly place them in harm's way with no ability to resist him. Ignorance was not a viable option, as his presence and power would leave them completely vulnerable (Ephesians 5:10-13).

DELIVERANCE FROM THE EVIL ONE

Satan is a diabolical enemy. He is not just any adversary but an opponent who has real power to destroy lives. He has been raging against God since the time of creation. According to Scripture, Satan was a particularly powerful and high-ranking angel who led an angelic host to rebel against God (Isaiah 14:12-14, Revelations 12:7-9). The Hebrew word for Satan means *adversary*. He has a number of designations, including the devil (Matthew 4:1), the serpent (Genesis 3:1; 2 Corinthians 11:3), the great dragon (Revelations 12:9), the prince of the power of the air (Ephesians 2:2), the god of this age (2 Corinthians 4:4), the evil one (Ephesians 6:16), the prince of demons (Matthew 12:24), the accuser (Revelations 12:10) and the tempter (Matthew 4:3, 1 Thessalonians 3:5). Satan was responsible for tempting Eve and then Adam to lure them both to disobey God. His temptations brought sin and death into the world. He corrupted humanity with evil and severed their relationship with their Creator through humanity's failure. He is the harbinger of the sin, suffering, and evil that has infected all of God's creation.

Humanity has been held prisoner under Satan's dominion (Colossians. 1:13). From a human perspective, he has been an unconquerable enemy who constantly leveraged the corruption in the world to bring darkness and destruction that has damaged human lives and God's creation (Romans 8:18-22). Satan's attack on Jesus was an attempt to take down God's champion, Jesus, who was sent to rescue humanity from their impossible bondage. His experience was a prophetic foretaste of the ongoing battle His followers would face, too. His success in overcoming this evil would be the basis for training His disciples to prepare for these future encounters with him. Teaching His men to pray was not about having a memorable quiet time; it was preparing them for spiritual warfare.

Jesus fully engaged in a visible conflict with Satan and his demons. Jesus's presence was a pivotal point in God's redemptive purpose. Jesus rescued vulnerable people afflicted by unclean spirits. He healed others of sicknesses from evil spirits. He cast out demons from those tormented and possessed by them. He delivered people from the active sufferings directly caused by Satan and his horde of fallen angels. Jesus stepped into the world of darkness and brought healing and freedom.

While Jesus delivered people from temporal afflictions, His ultimate purpose is to deliver people from the evil one. He came announcing that the kingdom of heaven was at hand. Satan had blinded the eyes of humanity and Israel to respond to it. Satan continues to heavily influence the values and beliefs of people. He corrupted the moral and spiritual well-being of humanity and God's chosen people, Israel.

The Pharisees accused Jesus of casting out demons by the power of Beelzebul, the prince of demons. They were blinded to the reality of their own Messiah, Jesus! Conversely, Jesus confronted the Pharisees and identified that Satan was their father because they refused to embrace Him (John 8:44). Jesus was constantly at war, fighting to rescue people from the influence of the evil one.

Jesus trained his disciples to stand against the devil. There were times He gave them the power to cast out demons and set people free from their affliction (Matthew 10:7-8). While this had enormous benefits to those delivered from many afflictions orchestrated by the devil, the greatest deliverance was not from the temporary circumstances of this world but the ultimate freedom of being reconciled to their heavenly Father. They could not follow Jesus without facing evil and the evil one. Asking the Father to deliver them from the evil one was a reminder to not underestimate their most powerful adversary because they were outmatched on their own. There were many responsibilities the Lord expected them to carry out, and there were other things that only God could do for them. They had to learn to take responsibility to stand against him, but they could only do this with God's help. Leading them into temptation was part of their training.

THE POWER OF GOD TO DELIVER HIS PEOPLE

But what did God's help look like? Some insight can be gained based on what the Father did for His Son's wilderness experience. The Father delighted in the Son and promised the power of His personal presence through this test. The second provision was His Word. It is worth noting what the Father did not do.

The Father did not supernaturally interfere in the testing of Jesus in the desert. He did nothing to mitigate the experience. He did not miraculously provide manna to feed him; He did not make water flow from rocks, and He did not send angels until after the temptations were over. One might conclude that the Father did nothing to help the Son. But if you reverse-engineer the experience, we see that Jesus took advantage of the Word from the Father to overcome the evil one. The Father's deliverance was the authority of His Word.

Every response Jesus had to every temptation was anchored to the Father's Word. He did not improvise, creatively argue with the devil, debate the issue, or compromise. His response was nothing more than the truth of God's Word. He knew it so well that He quoted it to the devil. But knowing God's Word is not the solution in and of itself. Even the devil quoted Scripture in the very act of tempting Jesus. What is even more important is the truth of God's Word clearly shaped His decisions and choices, even under enormous stress.

> "Therefore, everyone who hears these words of Mine, and acts upon them, may be compared to a wise man, who built his house upon the rock. And the rain descended, and the floods came, and the winds blew, and burst against that house; and yet it did not fall, for it had been founded upon the rock."
>
> Matthew 7:24-25, NASB 1977

Jesus trained the disciples that the most powerful way the Father would deliver them from the evil one was through His Word. This did not mean to say that the Father may, in various circumstances, intervene in the actions of evil and deliver them in a supernatural way. It did not preclude God from simply interjecting some unforeseen variable into any situation and changing the trajectory of events. The Father could send a person out of the blue to help rescue them from a crisis. God has no boundaries in providing for His children. But the most consistent and distinct way the Father delivers from any evil, specifically the evil one, is by building life on the unshakable foundation of the Word of God. This was the only solid foundation that can sustain us through every trial, temptation, and sacrifice in serving the Son.

While this may feel pedestrian or even boring to us now, this was life-giving to the disciples! The Father's Word, energized and driven home by the personal presence of the Holy Spirit, was the difference-maker in overcoming the attacks of evil or stumbling under the weight of his attacks. But when Jesus said God's Word would deliver them, He was not referring to being able to quote Scripture. Simply memorizing Scripture was not the way the Father delivered them from evil.

Certainly, passages like Psalm 1 indicate the supreme value of delighting in God's Word and meditating on it day and night (Psalm 1:2). But knowing the truth has always been distinguished from living truth. God's Word was not created by the imagination of mankind. It was the revealed will of God (2 Timothy 3:16). Human authors were directed and carried along by the Spirit of God to provide the divine integrity of God's revelation to His people (2 Timothy 3:16-17; 2 Peter 20-21). Jesus Himself was described as the living Word. He was the very expression of the Father's heart to Israel.

The Pharisees and Scribes had created traditions, regulations, and man-made rules that reflected a glimpse of God's truth but overwhelmed it with the teachings and doctrines of men (Colossians 2:21-22). In spite of this persistent disobedience to the Word, God pursued His people and gave them numerous opportunities to be rescued from evil.

Jesus's exact words were, "Everyone who hears these words of Mine, and acts upon them (Matthew 7:24)." This was the primary manner by which God delivered His people from the evil one. Doing what the Word says is the foundation for overcoming trials, temptations, and personal circumstances. Obedience to truth is the pathway to true victory. While this may appear a simple issue of common sense, obedience played two roles in Jesus's narrative.

Acting on Jesus's words is both proactive and preventative. Obedience builds the foundation for a solid and strong spiritual life. It is preventative because when the storms of life bring trials, temptations, and even evil, only a life trained on acting on Jesus's words produces a resilient, God-honoring response.

LEARNING TO BE DOERS OF THE WORD

Knowledge does not equal obedience. The Bible warns that knowledge makes us arrogant, but love edifies (1 Corinthians 8:1). James reiterates the warning: do not be hearers of the Word, but doers of the Word (James 1:22). To return to the text, the images of rain, floods, and storms reflect the inevitable abuse every house would experience from the elements. Jesus's point was these trials and temptations are the things that every person will face in life as routinely as rain and wind beat upon a house. Every person, and particularly any person who follows Jesus, will face the storms of trials and temptations. They are as common and persistent as the natural elements are with a physical dwelling.

Trials and temptations can produce patience that results in maturity. Building a house takes time, as does building one's life. There are many components that go into building a house. Since that process takes time and one is often preoccupied with the visible structure and not the foundation, the flaws and weaknesses of the foundation may not be seen for years.

In the face of one's most vulnerable moments in His life, the safety net is always God's Word. When a person finds discouragement to eliminate any hope of what is possible, God's Word provides that hope. When someone flounders over their own lack of perspective, the testimony from God provides that wisdom to keep moving. Knowing God's Word is indispensable, but choosing to obey God's truth is non-negotiable. If one is to build a spiritually solid life grounded on truth, the prerequisite is being doers of His Word. Everyone is responsible for building their own life because only the individual can choose to personalize truth and act upon it.

No one can obey God's Word for anyone else. Parents cannot make their children choose to act on God's Word. Spouses can't make spouses obey truth. Friends cannot force friends to be doers of the Word. The church cannot make anyone internalize truth and build their life on God's Word. Regardless of all the teaching, training, exhorting, and preaching, none of that guarantees obedience.

> "And everyone who hears these words of mine and does not do them will be like a foolish man who built his house on the sand. And the rain fell, and the floods came, and the winds blew and beat against that house, and it fell, and great was the fall of it."
>
> Matthew 7:26-27

We just had the wonderful privilege of having my son and his wife and our grandkids in town for the holidays. Our granddaughter just turned two years of age, and our grandson reached the one-year-old mark about a month ago. My son and family live with his in-laws as they work to secure their own home. We have always gone to see them over the past couple of years, but this year, we planned a Christmas surprise by having them fly out here for part of the holidays. This is the first time we have had the chance to hang with our grandkids in our own space. It was so fun to play with them, feed them, and interact with them. The older one has become much more interactive as she is at the age of formulating sentences and talking back to us. But we also remember that while they were pretty good at doing what Mom and Dad asked them to do, there were times that did not happen.

Our grandson had a delightful habit of taking his fork and slamming it on the plate in front of him as vigorously as possible.

Mom and Dad did all they could to coach our little grandson to stop beating his plate like he was beating a drum. They finally had to take the fork away before he stabbed himself in the eye or broke the plate. Our grandkids are little, but they still need to learn to obey their mom and dad.

You have to see how critically important this complementary statement was from Jesus. While it may seem obvious, He would include the flip side of those who do not obey His words. He explained the obvious, and to do such a thing intuitively tells us that Jesus was trying to make a definitive point.

HOW TO BUILD YOUR LIFE TO FAIL

A house falling under the weight of the storms of life is a vivid description of the inevitable fall of one who does not act on the words of Jesus. The picture is identical to the wise man who built his house on the rock with the unfortunate distinction that the foundation was sand. The storms and winds did not cause the house to become weak; the storms exposed the weakness of the foundation. When people hear, meditate, reflect, and muse over God's Word but never get around to obeying that truth, they are building their house on the sand.

People can give every appearance they are building their life on God's Word when they are just going through the motions. Anyone can grow up in a Christian home, attend church, participate in children and youth programs, and get involved in serving as an adult. They may attend a small group, give help to a special project, and appear to be highly involved. But coming to a church does not make one a Christian any more than standing in a garage makes someone a mechanic. When a storm hits a person, and they have not been acting on the words of Jesus, according to His own words, the collapse is inevitable and catastrophic.

This spiritual collapse of one's life produces unique collateral damage. Having an appearance of godliness but denying the power of it forces one's faith to collapse. Nothing could be more devastating than the foundation they thought they were building on was actually sand. The erosion can be gradual or sudden, but the end result is gripping. Those who are on the wide path may find various destructive experiences throughout their lifetime, mostly because of creating a pathway that implodes on itself. False prophets will be found out because the fruit of their life does not match their truth claim. Unfortunately, for those who have a works-based idea of salvation, their house will fall when they stand before Jesus. The obvious debate in this case swirls around the question of whether a person was ever a true disciple of Jesus or lost their salvation because of this obvious collapse. If your imagination is captured by the contextual narrative, you will discover two things.

Jesus already warned about false prophets who look authentic but are actually "ravenous wolves." Their true nature was to be revealed by the fruit of their life (Matthew 7:15-16). In this case, these individuals are not true followers of Christ, regardless of their outward appearance. He also warned of individuals who claimed to prophesy in Jesus's name, cast out demons, and did mighty works to serve Jesus. But they are rejected by Christ and driven from His presence because, according to Jesus, He does not know them.

There is no resume that anyone can submit to God to prove their own worthiness to be a true citizen of God's kingdom. Conversely, the language of Jesus stated even a more sobering criterion. The ultimate reality of citizenship was not the individual's claim to know Jesus but if Jesus knew them. The apostle Paul reiterated the same principle in his letter to the Galatians:

"But now that you have come to know God, or rather to be known by God, how can you turn back again to the weak and worthless elementary principles of the world, whose slaves you want to be once more? You observe days and months and seasons and years! I am afraid I may have labored over you in vain (Galatians 4:9-11)."

Jesus taught His disciples about how to live under the leadership of their heavenly Father. The nature of His teaching was directed to how the disciples operate in the context of being part of God's family, called to seek first His kingdom and His righteousness. The danger for true believers was becoming a victim of trials, temptations, and the evil one. Satan has always been committed to undermining every follower of Christ, taking them off mission, and becoming overwhelmed. His goal is to disillusion believers with the hypocrisy of religion. The devil wants to discourage Christ's followers from living on mission in the face of cultural wars over discrimination and prejudice. He desires us to place personal preferences above kingdom purpose. Any degree of separation from the Father's call is success in his mind.

This would certainly rupture our confidence in God's sovereign provision and participation in their lives. Any trial, tragedy, or temptation can blindside us at any stage of life, depending on the storm that hits us. The greater danger for every child of God is not losing their salvation but being disqualified from His blessing because of the attack of the devil and the destruction He brings. Like Job, the key is not whether we can spot Satan at work in our circumstances as much as keeping our eye on our heavenly Father, regardless of the circumstances.

People who lose a parent at a young age might become angry at God because they think He should have prevented it. Someone who loses a job for unjust reasons might be embittered and lose faith because their personal self-worth has not been anchored to what their heavenly Father says about them. Others believe God should be a concierge who serves them rather than joining Him in the work He is doing. These storms can collapse on life at any phase: teenager, young adult, or even later in years. If a person has not been training their senses through obedience to God's truth, the problem of evil can destroy their confidence in the integrity of God's care for them.

There are many ways that one does not act on Jesus' words. Obviously, all options result in the same outcome: not doing what Jesus taught. But there are some spiritual traps that disciples can fall into when it comes to falling into the deception of not obeying Christ.

Everyone needs to be reminded that failing to obey Jesus is disobedience by omission. Most have experienced disobedience by ignorance. Neglect may be a more "acceptable" form of disobedience. But, like a parent asking their children to obey, our heavenly Father expects His children to do as He instructs. A good parent teaches their children about life, and their wisdom is critical for raising a boy to become a godly man or a girl to become a woman of righteousness.

THE POWER OF UNSEEN GRACE

Jesus continually provided grace for His disciples. Grace is the kindness of God to provide what is both necessary and sufficient for life in Christ and godliness. His Word has always been a foundational expression of His grace. For those who act upon His words, His grace was the substance of a transformed life. But He also offered grace to those who did not keep His words. Grace was pervasive in His actions towards His people regardless of old or new covenant. Like His Father's posture toward Israel, Jesus extended patience and grace to His disciples because it has always been indispensable in God's relationship with His people.

However, grace can be abused. Paul dealt with this when some suggested that if God's grace abounds in the face of our sin, we should continue to sin so that grace may abound more (Romans 6:1-2). When people intentionally disobey God, they often accuse others of not showing them grace. Grace becomes a shield to protect them from individuals who confront them about the hypocrisy of their disobedience. Grace is often disguised as patience, love, and even forgiveness, but inevitably, the appeal is for tolerance to avoid dealing with the truth of disobedience.

Grace teaches God's people to deny ungodliness and worldly desires and to live righteously and godly (Titus 2:11-12). God's grace flourishes in brokenness and helplessness because it always compels people back to the Father's forgiveness and hope for new life, especially in the face of their own failure. The heartbeat of godly sorrow is repentance that leads to salvation *without regret*, especially in contrast to worldly sorrow that produces death (2 Corinthians 7:9-10). When God's people crumble under testing, falter under the weight of suffering, or succumb to temptations, our heavenly Father's loyal love constantly pursues His children because He is a forgiving Father.

FAITH AND FAILURE

At one time or another, everyone feels their failure is unrecoverable. Sometimes, people feel this way because of what they lose, such as a job, a marriage, a position, a responsibility, or several other staples of life. Sometimes, their failure feels unrecoverable because of the damage it causes in other people's lives. Family, friends, church community, or even work or neighborhood can be affected. Most are ashamed of their actions and would rather run and hide than be labeled as that person who failed.

Some may not care that God forgives them because they are convinced their sin is unforgivable. But often, that is the evaluation of broken humanity, not a holy God. Often, the barrier is shame, fear, and pride. But when we truly understand and embrace His forgiveness, we can trust that He will step into the gap between our failure and His purpose and continue to lead us forward.

The temptation in our Christian walk is to passively affirm truth without obeying it. Truth becomes inspirational, not transformational. The principles of God's Word become nothing more than part of an eclectic library of self-help ideas to use when it is convenient or obviously relevant. However, connecting truth to real life is often obliterated by the deception that we have sole authority over the direction of our own lives. Instead of submitting to our heavenly Father, we usurp His authority to decide for ourselves.

TRUE FREEDOM

One step further along this line of thinking has become the masterful art of reinterpreting Scriptures. Not acting on Jesus's words takes another degree of separation from truth, where individuals reinterpret the text to fit their behavior, rather than repenting of behavior to fit the text.

Interpreting the Scriptures has always been challenging and never perfected, but the reality in our world is that people will not endure sound doctrine and will gradually abandon it to hear ideas that suit their own desires. Truth will be exchanged for myths (2 Timothy 4:3-4). Under the noble umbrella for greater clarity surfaces greater confusion over the text. There is no greater danger than a disciple who fails to value how vital God's Word is in delivering him or her from the evil one.

Christ's words are indispensable to building a life that remains firmly rooted in a relationship with the Father and in fellowship with Christ. God's Word, more often than not, is the answer to most of our prayers. We often want God to fix the circumstances in our lives rather than be faithful through the circumstances of life. We ask God to remove the burdens rather than believing the power of His presence to sustain us through the burden. We wonder if God still loves us when He is asking if we still love Him.

Knowing God's Word without the power of the personal presence of the Spirit of God also becomes self-destructive. Too many people have memorized God's Word, but it has remained essentially dormant on the back burner of their minds without ever effectively being imprinted into hearts and lives by the Spirit of God. If the Spirit of God was essential to Jesus's experience in the wilderness, it is indispensable to His followers. One without the other leaves a person building their life with an invisible, spiritual booby-trap that will cause collapse later. While it appears all the ingredients are present, it is like trying to make concrete without cement or water. One missing ingredient will undermine the strength of the final product, and Jesus warned that the same would happen to them, apart from *acting on His words*.

PRINCIPLES ABOUT BEING DELIVERED FROM THE EVIL ONE:

1. The single, most powerful way God delivers His children from evil is through the power of His Word.

   - How would you evaluate your history in obeying God's Word as opposed to just being a hearer of the Word? Can you be honest about this?
   - How much do you feel you have a love for God's Word? What does that look like?

2. We keep pleading with God to change our circumstances and have often failed to see how God has been using our circumstances to change our character.

   - How do you identify the working of God in your circumstances?
   - How do you rely on your relationship with the Lord when life is difficult?

3. The key to being delivered from evil is a call from Christ to hear His words and act upon them. Being doers of the Word is far more important than how many verses you have memorized.

   - When was the last time you specifically obeyed a truth from God's Word that changed your behavior in any given circumstance?
   - Do you memorize Scripture, and why do you spend time in this discipline?

4. Memorizing truth may take talent, but obeying truth transforms the heart.

   - How much do you feel God's truth transforms your beliefs and values?

- What examples from your own life could you share with someone about how you obey truth?

PRAYER

Heavenly Father, I want to live my life on the foundation of your truth and word. True transformation comes when I choose to make decisions based on actual truth, not just spiritual ideas and concepts. Continue to use everything and anything in my life to train me to embrace godly character with the discernment to honor you even in the face of evil.

Help me to spend more time listening to the Holy Spirit as He connects the truth of your Word to the real situations in my daily life. Forgive me for being so distracted in building my house on sand rather than on the foundation of your words.

Help me see the power of your Word in my life and give me the courage to help others see in me a genuine attraction to Christ. Amen.

CHAPTER 11

DON'T FORGET THIS

Why this Prayer Changes Everything for you!

My daughter is getting married to a fabulous young man who loves the Lord this summer. Like every other couple, the anticipation of their wedding day starts to be overwhelmed by the mountain of planning and details that go into the planning. They are facing the strain of who to be involved in the wedding party, what friends to invite, and who they cannot invite. The details of food, decorations, venues, and service details can become very tedious. The stress couples experience is often overwhelming.

I counseled my daughter exactly the same way that I have coached many other couples. In spite of the massive amount of planning, only about three or four essentials have to be considered for a wedding. You need a pastor, a couple to exchange vows, and two witnesses to sign off on the legal component of the marriage – that is it! If we had those three things, we could have a successful ceremony. Everything else is nice and desirable and adds to the celebration, but they are not indispensable to getting married. They are all cultural practices that make the day special. My advice is: Do not let all the nice things ruin the essential things. Keeping the right perspective is critical to not allowing the desirable things to ruin the celebration of the main thing.

The whole nature of the Lord's Prayer is that it was given as a spiritual blueprint for a God-honoring life. It begins with understanding the relationship with our heavenly Father. Among all the other attributes that His disciples need to hold dearly, one of the most critical to remember is the Father's forgiveness. Since He delights in His children, He eagerly forgives His children who understand the eternal weight of such mercy.

The counterbalance for any potential abuse of the Father's generosity to forgive is the posture of humility under the shadow of His holiness. God's holiness prevents any selfish inclination to exploit His mercy for worldly pursuits. The primary motivation for the disciples was for their Father's namesake. His men were learning what God expected of them was to honor His name, not promote their reputation.

The defining purpose for our lives is His coming kingdom and doing His will on earth as it is in heaven. In order to even begin this process, Jesus taught that we need to value eternal things and to be so heavenly minded so that we become useful to Him here on earth. But we must also keep our eyes firmly fixed on our relationship with Him. With so many distractions in life, this has become an enormous struggle for most. The secret to commitment is when we store up treasures in heaven and keep our eyes fixed on things above, the inevitable result will be genuine commitment motivated by love. There are lots of things we value, but if we are distracted and have our eyes on other things, then our love for Christ will be something we do when we have time rather than our passion for everything we do.

Anxiety is one of the most corrosive, debilitating infections with which a believer can live. What complicates this is it always seems to be an unpredictable reaction to life over which we have little or no control. Yet, often, our worries are about far grander things than our basic needs in life. Jesus commanded His disciples to trust the Father for daily needs. This is the only part of the Lord's Prayer and His commentary in which Jesus specifically points out the importance of faith. Without faith, it is inevitable that worry and anxiety will undermine God's work in our lives. Faith and confidence in our heavenly Father is the solution to anxiety, and anxiety is the predominant enemy of faith.

People who can truly trust their Father are passionate about His kingdom work and His righteousness. The disciples are called to put the same kind of effort into God's kingdom as the Gentiles do in stockpiling their earthly goods and treasures. The true mark of a faithful believer is their commitment to the gospel of the kingdom and living in a manner that honors their Father who is in heaven.

Forgiveness is a powerful element for the child of God. The believer that fails to understand forgiveness fails to understand the heart of their Father. Nothing provides greater refuge and freedom than those who have learned to forgive others. The basis for forgiveness is inseparably grounded in the Father's forgiveness for the child of God. Therefore, the willingness of the child of God to forgive others says more about what they believe God will do for them than what others have done to them.

Forgiveness is so critical to kingdom life that Jesus took the time to explain the essential danger of an unforgiving spirit. Unforgiveness will always be a breeding ground for anger, resentment, and bitterness. The longer a person hangs on to a spirit of unforgiveness, the more dangerous they become to others. He taught that unforgiveness produces judgmentalism. This produces a censorious attitude towards others in the community of faith, resulting in complaining, criticizing, and condemning others for even the littlest imperfections in their life. If left unchecked, unforgiveness has the capacity to even blaspheme God's holy name in front of unbelievers, undermine God's kingdom work, and destroy any claim to being righteous or serving a righteous God. When unbelievers see this kind of hypocrisy, they will be rightly outraged at any Christians who act so contrary to the character of who we claim God to be, and they will trample on everything that we hold dear.

Forgiveness is the doorway to healing and freedom. The solution to the bitterness, anger, and toxic waste of unforgiveness is forgiveness. The ultimate pathway to healing is to forgive, and healing can never be complete without forgiveness. Forgiveness is costly because it agrees to live with the consequences of other people's actions and trust that our heavenly Father will bring true justice to sin in His time and purpose.

But the one who forgives must also be convinced that God has his or her back, that He will stand in that gap of what he or she lost, and provide for him or her moving forward. If a child of God does not believe that God has his or her best interest at heart and that He can work all things together for good for those who love Him, then forgiveness is virtually impossible. Bitterness not only flows out of the event of being wronged, but it can be energized by the permanent loss of what that person hoped would be in the future. The bottom-line principle is more appropriate for this issue than any other that we may choose to apply it – however you want people to treat you, so treat them.

Asking the Father not to lead us into temptation is actually a request not to allow extreme testing that could change the trajectory of one's life, even in victory. This experience may not be anything we would wish on our worst enemy, but God may choose to train and equip you for something more profound in the future. These tests or temptations can be severe and even involve the devil, but God's desire is always to affirm His children and their faith and character in a sinful world.

There are three critical temptations every child of God needs to learn to address:

Walking the narrow way of His kingdom and His righteousness versus the broad way that most walk.

- The prayer itself defines the substance of the narrow way, and these pathways are journeys of the heart more than anything else.
- False prophets who appear to serve God but do not faithfully communicate His Word have been a danger since the beginning of time. Holding faithfully to the revealed Word of God clearly defines the life of a true believer in Christ.
- The final temptation is best described as a performance-based salvation. The basic distinction is those who are religious but do not have a genuine relationship with the Father. Religion is often the broad way disguised as God's way and avoids the essence of salvation, which is a relationship with the Father through Christ.

These three are the temptations that God may lead us to face and address to grow our faith, deepen our commitment, and refine our character. He does not need good people, but He needs godly people who are devoted to Christ.

Finally, Jesus gave the perfect solution to deliver us from the evil one. The key to deliverance is the power of God's Word. There has never been a substitute for the words of Christ, but the age-old warning back then is exactly the same warning we must heed now. Hearers of the word who are not doers of the word delude themselves, and their faith is worthless. Only those who hear and act on His words build a life that will stand against life's storms, regardless of hardships, trials, or temptations. God's provision is completely sufficient for His children to live a spirit-filled, God-honoring life.

WHAT JESUS DID NOT ADDRESS

Finally, notice what Jesus did not discuss in His prayer or in His commentary on His prayer. This spiritual blueprint is designed to help anyone overcome the discouragement of broken relationships, the disappointment of church conflict, and the hypocrisy of moral failures. He did not discuss many things that are often a huge distraction in the modern-day church.

Jesus did not talk about leadership, roles, or responsibilities of men or women. He did not try to address equality or social justice issues. He did not address cultural ideology or the global economy. Jesus did not speak to rights and freedoms, nor did He try to address politics or the economy. He does not speak about citizenship and how to address governments, and He does not speak about ethnic discrimination. This is not to say that these are unimportant issues by any means, but the toxic nature of our world has tempted people to abandon the foundational blueprint of a God-honoring life to champion many other important issues, but not from the foundation or perspective of the blueprint of the Lord's Prayer.

Many have stepped off this platform and adopted their personal conviction grounded in a first-world ideology. Again, there is nothing wrong with addressing issues that are critical needs in our world that expose the raw nerve of God's creation, ultimately damaged by sin and evil. But like the instructions from stewards on an airplane, if there is an emergency, you must put your oxygen mask on before you help anyone else. You may not be able to help anyone if you do not take the proper precautions to stay healthy and spiritually alert yourself. The Lord's Prayer is the spiritual oxygen mask that we must put on first before we can address these other critical issues, or we may not be any good to anyone.

Jesus did not talk about spiritual gifts, positions in the church, ministry programs, mission strategies, or marketing tools. While some of these are obviously addressed in other New Testament books, they are not necessary to understand how to live a God-honoring life. We encourage people to know and use their gifts, but they are not the first priority to living a Spirit-filled, God-honoring life. Jesus wanted a transformed life, driven by a loving relationship with the Father and desiring to be part of the most exhilarating adventure known to man – the gospel of Jesus.

Jesus did not talk about the church, programming, ministries, buildings, or financial concerns either. He did not speak about mission boards, global partners, affiliations, denominations, or networks. Of course, this may sound silly because these are all the realities of our existence. We need to return to those things Jesus taught His men in a simple but deeply profound prayer designed to teach them how to live a Spirit-filled, God-honoring, powerful life in relationship to their heavenly Father at the invitation of Jesus Himself.

Obviously, one will argue there would be no point in speaking about things that have not even come into being. But the more profound and powerful point is that living a godly life is not about an institution, programs, branding, website, the size of the church, or financial budgets. Those are all part of our modern-day church both here and around the world to one degree or another. But none of those things, according to Jesus, is integral to the foundational blueprint for seeking His kingdom and living according to His righteousness.

This is precisely what has gone wrong with many believers. We have become enamored by the good things we think we should do because they are part of our cultural expectations of church, but we have forgotten the absolute essentials of what we must do. Our distractions with what we think we must have often replaced the spiritual blueprint of what Jesus said we must do.

If you have been stumbling over the discouragement of the institutionalized church, you may have good reasons. But learn to live a spiritually vitalized life because of your relationship with your heavenly Father, not because of the apparent hypocrisy you see around you. If Jesus has called us to live in the hostility of a world dominated by the evil one, surely we can extend His grace to the body of Christ, for whom He died and shed His blood.

PRINCIPLES ABOUT LIVING BY THE SPIRITUAL BLUEPRINT OF THE LORD'S PRAYER:

1. The Lord's Prayer is a spiritual blueprint for a God-honoring life.

2. Relationship with God always precedes responsibility. The three most important truths about our relationship with Him are that He is our heavenly Father, He forgives, and He requires humility from His people.

3. God's kingdom requires us to value eternal things and fix our eyes on His will in order to realize any commitment to serving His purposes here on earth.

4. Nothing can be more distracting to seeking God's kingdom and righteousness than this world's anxieties.

5. The most dangerous spiritual contagion in the Christian life is a spirit of unforgiveness.

6. My willingness to forgive says more about what I believe God can do for me than what others have done to me.

7. God never intended for my life to be lived in a vacuum. He may place me in a context where I face temptation in order to teach me how to resist the devil and develop a godly character.

8. God's greatest provision to deliver us from evil is through the power of His Word.

PRAY THEN LIKE THIS:

"Our Father in heaven,
hallowed be your name.

Your kingdom come,
your will be done, on earth as it is in heaven.

Give us this day our daily bread,

and forgive us our debts,
as we also have forgiven our debtors.

And lead us not into temptation,
but deliver us from evil.